HOLDING UP THE PROPHET'S HAND

HOLDING UP THE PROPHET'S HAND

SUPPORTING CHURCH WORKERS

BRUCE M. HARTUNG

CONCORDIA PUBLISHING HOUSE · SAINT LOUIS

Published by Concordia Publishing House
3558 S. Jefferson Avenue, St. Louis, MO 63118-3968
1-800-325-3040 • www.cph.org

Manufactured in the United States of America

Library of Congress Cataloging-in-Publication Data
Hartung, Bruce M.
  Holding up the prophet's hand : supporting church workers / Bruce M. Hartung.
        p.   cm.
        ISBN-13: 978-0-7586-0548-1
        ISBN-10: 0-7586-0548-X
    1. Church work. 2. Church officers. I. Title.
  BV683.H37 2011
  253'.2--dc23
  2011   026258

1 2 3 4 5 6 7 8 9 10   20 19 18 17 16 15 14 13 12 11

CONTENTS

WHY WORKER HEALTH MATTERS

Why write a book specifically on supporting church workers? Do church workers as a group need special attention?

In a word, yes. I am convinced of the need for special attention because I see church workers at increased risk of sadness, despair, stress, frustration, cynicism, anger, and disappointment. For a number of reasons, church workers living out this vocation are at much more risk than many other folks. The risk comes from several sources.

First, people-oriented professions carry specific, inherent vocational risks. Like counselors, social workers, nurses, teachers, and other caregivers, church workers face stressors common to the helping professions. Day by day, these workers deal with the crises of others—unemployment, financial distress, personal illnesses, and the death of loved ones. Professionals called to help others during stressful circumstances find these circumstances upping the stress ante in their own lives too.

Second, stress often increases when one's vocation asks the worker to connect challenging human experiences with the Gospel of Jesus Christ. I will have much more to say about this throughout the book.

Third, church workers most often have personal relationships with those they serve. Unlike counselors, whose clients come and go, or firefighters, who meet emergency needs and then leave the scene, church workers walk closely with those they serve in day-by-day, ongoing relationships. In short, church workers meet more than the average number of life-stressors because of their people-oriented vocation. They minister to those they care about on a personal as well as professional level, often during times of crises.

Finally, they are called by God to apply the Gospel to the most daunting of human experiences. Is it any wonder that church workers sometimes succumb to dramatic risks of body, spirit, and self?

In the chapters of this section, I will focus on four crucial arenas: (1) satanic attack and spiritual warfare, (2) psychological stressors and stress, (3) burnout, and (4) secondary traumatic stress. Each is key as congregations seek to support their workers. However, readers will not find solutions to these challenges in Section 1. That is the task of the remaining sections of the book. Section 1 seeks simply to define and communicate the challenges in detail.

CHAPTER ONE

SATAN'S STRATEGY

Be sober-minded; be watchful. Your adversary the devil prowls around like a roaring lion, seeking someone to devour. (1 Peter 5:8)

I begin with a fable. I begin in this way not to be dramatic but because I want to make and underscore an important point. I wholeheartedly believe that the devil does indeed prowl on earth like a roaring lion, just as Scripture says (1 Peter 5:8). I do believe the devil and his demons seek to undermine the work of the Christian Church.

■ ■ ■ ■ ■

"This may be the day the Lord has made," thought Satan as he sped from the garden and back toward Hades, "but it was a great day for me anyway."

An easy smile came to Satan's face. He had just completed his successful temptation of Adam and Eve, destroying the bliss of the garden, and unleashing sin and death into God's good creation. "What a great day!" he repeated to himself.

A hellish crowd awaited Evil's triumphant return. But no sooner had the applause died down than Satan called together his lieutenants. "We must make further plans," Satan announced. "There will be many more opportunities. We must use our resources effectively. Any ideas?"

One of Satan's lieutenants cleared his throat. Those around the table leaned forward in anticipation. "We assume," he began, "that there will be followers of God—people of the light. He has promised a Savior. And He will keep that promise. These people will seek one another out. They will gather and form groups, clusters, organizations made up of people whom our Enemy will rescue. In these groups, leaders will arise. If we can get to the leaders, we can undercut and destroy the efforts of the groups."

"Interesting," said Satan after thoughtful silence, "Tell me more."

"We weaken and take down the God-followers by attacking their leaders, and this is how we do it. We begin by creating stress and trouble in their lives. We beat them down. We find ways to cause them to lose heart. We work to isolate the leaders from one another and from the people they serve. We tempt them to feel that they are carrying their burdens alone. Then we instigate undercurrents of jealousy and discontent, shame and denial, criticism and gossip throughout each group."

Murmurs of approval spread through the assembled demonic army.

Another lieutenant continued, "And we can work on the God-followers too. We will keep them distracted from thinking about their leaders' needs. We will distract them with their own stress and worries. And when they make the effort to demonstrate any kind of care for their leaders, we will stir up conflict around every little thing and distract them some more."

Satan thought about the plan. "If we get to the leaders,"

he said, "we can undercut their effectiveness and the influence of all the God-followers. We'll isolate the leaders, criticize them, isolate them, overwork them, and demoralize them. Yes! That will be the plan!"

Someone cheered. Then, two more. Someone began to clap and the applause became a crescendo. When it finally died down, Satan continued, "Keep the married ones from spending time with their spouses! Keep them from taking care of their bodies! Convince them they have so much work to do they have no time for exercise, adequate sleep, a healthful diet, or personal time in fellowship with their God."

The applause began anew, soon becoming a roar. Satan shouted over it:

"Encourage conflict as it simmers underground. Cause hard feelings and break up relationships. Isolate them! Attack them! Isolate them! Discourage them! Isolate them! Keep them away from anything that will comfort or nourish them—physically, emotionally, intellectually, or spiritually! Isolate them! That is the plan."

All hell roared at these words. Satan's followers hoisted him onto their shoulders in celebration of their anticipated victory. Soon they would deploy to carry out his plan. But for now, they celebrated.

■ ■ ■ ■ ■

And that is Satan's plan. If I were to create a game plan focused on undermining the work of the Church begun by our Lord Jesus Christ, I would unleash that attack in the following order:

First, I would seek to destroy the significant relationships of church workers, their relationships with their spouses, children, friends, co-workers, parish leaders, congregation members and even other church workers.

Second, I would work to destroy the relationships of congregation members with one another, isolating them and fracturing community.

Third, I would cause the faithful to question their beliefs.

As I've ministered to church leaders over the years, I have seen Satan use these

IT IS VITAL THAT CHRISTIANS RECOGNIZE OUR ENEMY AND DISCERN HIS STRATEGY.

three steps again and again. And sadly, his strategy often works! Armies that hope to fight successfully must be able to identify the enemy. In the same way, it is vital that Christians recognize our enemy and discern his strategy. St. Paul was certainly on target:

> Finally, be strong in the Lord and in the strength of His might. Put on the whole armor of God, that you may be able to stand against the schemes of the devil. For we do not wrestle against flesh and blood, but against the rulers, against the authorities, against the cosmic powers over this present darkness, against the spiritual forces of evil in the heavenly places. Therefore take up the whole armor of God, that you may be able to withstand in the evil day, and having done all, to stand firm. (Ephesians 6:10–13)

Because a church worker's vocation is to connect people

to the saving Gospel of Jesus Christ, they are exceptionally vulnerable to Satan's attack. Were a parochial school math teacher, for instance, to confine herself solely to her academic subject without any concern for the spiritual lives of her students, she would likely be less vulnerable to satanic attack. Her activities would be simply less threatening to the kingdom of darkness.

However, a math teacher who connects with her students on a spiritual level does threaten the satanic game plan. If she connects on a spiritual level with the families of her students, she poses even more of a threat. Likewise, a pastor who offers only theological abstractions in his teaching and preaching may not find himself in Satan's crosshairs. But if that teaching, preaching, and counseling links the Gospel of Christ to his hearers' lives, then his work poses more of a threat to the satanic game plan. If that pastor grows relationally close to his people, caring for them on a personal as well as a professional level, that threat increases more.

In short, when church workers do what a congregation calls them to do, that is, integrate their daily leadership tasks with the Gospel of Jesus Christ they proclaim, they put themselves in a much more dangerous position. Congregations need to understand that we ask our workers to assume a higher risk, spiritually speaking. Understanding it, we must faithfully take up the task of supporting our workers.

Church workers, along with all those who seek to connect the Gospel daily, are by virtue of their vocation, in positions of special vulnerability for satanic attack.

It is unsettling to think of our parishes as places of spiritual warfare. We would rather consider the church as a place of respite, of safety. There, we hear God's Word. There, we receive the Sacraments and support one another as members of the Body of Christ. However, the power of the Word and Sacraments make the congregation and its leaders targets for special attack.

John Kleinig notes the dangers seminarians and seminary faculties face:

> If we heed what Luther has to say about the role of the devil in the spiritual formation of theologian, we will realize our seminaries are spiritual battlegrounds, contested places, rather than spiritual oases, places of refuge from temptation. We will also be able to help our students understand why they and their families come under such concerted attack at certain points during their course of study.[1]

Read that quote again, substituting "congregations" for "seminaries." It fits! When a congregation does the work of the Gospel—proclaiming the Gospel in the human condition—it also places itself in greater danger. Congregations content to focus only on themselves pose less danger to the kingdom of darkness than those who intentionally become more robust in their outreach.

The general principle, then, holds true for both individuals and congregations: the more we work to connect the Gospel to the lives of individuals, organizations, and our community, the more risk we assume. Attention to this reality will motivate congregations to do all they can to shield and support their workers. Martin Luther helps us understand this:

> It is impossible to keep the devil from shooting evil thoughts and lusts into your heart. But see to it that you do not let such arrows (Eph. 6:16) stick there and take root, but tear them out and throw them away. Do what one of the ancient fathers counseled long ago: "I cannot," he said, "keep a bird from flying over my head. But I can certainly keep it from nesting in my hair or from biting my nose off."[2]

SPEAKING PERSONALLY

Is all this talk about Satan and his minions anachronistic? Hopelessly out of date? It may seem so, given the fact that Western culture today denies not only the power but also the existence of Satan and his demons. Yet true danger lies in the offhand dismissal of evil. We need not deny Satan's existence. We need only ignore it. We need only to disregard it. We need only to shrug off Satan's strategic opposition to the plan of salvation flowing from the goodness of God and from His Christ.

When I was a full-time pastoral counselor, I often saw the results of evil in the lives of those I counseled. But frankly, if pressed, I might have waffled on the question of whether or not Satan was, even in part, responsible. Then I was called to serve at the national headquarters of The Lutheran Church—Missouri Synod. I was on staff for only a few months before I saw the evidence of Satan actively attacking the very foundations of countless local congregations as well as the Synod itself. I began to realize that Satan's primary tactic involves influencing the ways people in those congregations, and in the church as a whole, behave toward one another.

To para-phrase Luther, the devil is not silly enough to 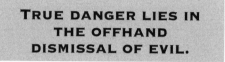 tempt us to think or act in ways that even unbelievers understand as wrong and sinful. Rather, in the Church, Satan disguises himself, using religious language on the lips of some to destroy others, to exert power and control over them, to abuse them. This is a version of the adage that righteous ends justify any means.

Satan is real, and his aim is to destroy the witness of every church worker and every congregation. Dismissing this reality as fanciful, far-fetched, or delusional plays into his plans. Church workers and lay leaders alike make themselves vulnerable to his attacks by forgetting or ignoring this scriptural truth. Having seen again and again the corrosive behaviors of the baptized toward one another, I have no other explanation. Satan is at work.

TRUE DANGER LIES IN THE OFFHAND DISMISSAL OF EVIL.

CHAPTER TWO

STRESSORS AND STRESS

In the natural course of life, people encounter stressors of all kinds. We perceive stressful experiences as either negative or positive, depending on our capacity to cope with them. We experience stress in a positive way (*eustress*) when our health and performance enable us to rise to the occasion. For example, when we exercise at an optimal level, we stress our body's physical capacity. Then, after time on the treadmill or hiking trail, we rest by napping or by just sitting down and putting our feet up.

In contrast, we may experience stress in a negative way (*distress*) when the challenges we face appear too large. For example, perhaps a deadline looms and challenges our coping capacity. When we complete the task, the distress lifts.

When someone says, "I am stressed," they usually mean they are experiencing stress in a negative way, that the stress in their lives at that moment threatens their capacity to cope with it. Too much stress and a person shorts out. Too little stress and a person withers away. The ideal, of course, is to manage stress in ways that are optimal for one's well-being.

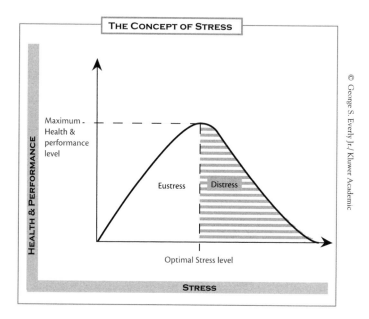

THE CONCEPT OF STRESS

© George S. Everly Jr./ Kluwer Academic

Maximum Health & performance level

Eustress

Distress

Optimal Stress level

HEALTH & PERFORMANCE

STRESS

This figure graphically shows the relationship between stress arousal (horizontal axis) and performance (vertical axis). As stress increases, so does performance (eustress). At the optimal stress level, performance has reached its maximum level. If stress continues to increase into the "distress" region, performance quickly declines. Should stress levels remain excessive, health will begin to erode as well.[1]

We deliberately choose some stressors. A director of Christian education might choose to exercise three times a week for an hour and a half because he believes that putting that kind of stress on his body will enhance his long-term health. A college senior may choose to add the stressors inherent in four years of additional study at the seminary because he believes God is calling him to become a pastor.

While we choose some stressors, others are just givens in life. A pastor may experience stress both in the preparation of each weekly sermon and its delivery. A teacher may experience stress both in preparing and then teaching her daily lesson plans. A deaconess may experience stress as she thinks about the four calls she has scheduled today in the homes of members struggling with significant illness.

Seldom are stressors, either chosen or given, the major issue for church workers. Stressors are simply part of the vocational life and circumstance of the church worker. The stressor is often a given; the stress response is, however, something that can be moderated or managed. How we manage stressors determines the effects on our body, mind, and spirit. Recent research highlights the drastic effects sudden distress can cause.

Clinicians and researchers alike have begun to accumulate evidence that sudden emotional stress can cause heart failure. In a syndrome no one yet fully understands, extreme grief, fear, anger, or shock can cause sudden death in generally healthy individuals with no prior history of heart disease. Doctors have nicknamed this "broken heart syndrome." They suggest that in rare cases people may literally be scared to death or die from sorrow.

Typically, however, distress works its damage more slowly. To understand how that happens, it's helpful to understand the process by which individuals deal with stress in a healthy way. First, when a perceived threat arises, the body gears up for action—fight or flight. Experts have identified a number of important changes that occur in our bodies when we feel endangered:

- Sugars, fats, and proteins are released for energy.
- Increased breathing rate brings in oxygen to "burn" fuel.
- Heartbeat and blood pressure increase; blood vessels expand, more blood is pumped to hard-working muscles.
- As workload increases, heat is carried away through breathing and perspiration.
- Nonessential functions are reduced, including gastro-intestinal activity and blood flow to the skin.
- To prepare for possible injury and bleeding, surface blood vessels constrict, and clotting substances are released into the blood (for scarring).
- The immune system becomes more active to prepare for infection, or becomes less active to reduce the inflammation and conserve energy.
- The brain's painkillers, *endorphins*, minimize the distracting discomfort of injury.
- Muscle tone increases, eye pupils enlarge (letting more light in), palms and feet become moist (increasing grip and traction)—all enhancing one's ability to engage in vigorous physical activity.[2]

Ideally, when the immediate threat disappears, our bodies relax and the factors listed above return to normal.[3] The movement back and forth, from gearing up to settling down, from warming up to cooling down, from feeling challenged to being relaxed, is a natural sequence, a typical pattern in a healthy life.

Thus, as a deaconess makes a hospital call, her blood pressure may increase as she focuses on the task at hand and the relationship to be served. When she completes the call and leaves the hospital, her blood pressure should decrease and her heart rate return to a lower level. In doing so, her body readies itself for the next activity. But something else has happened—she has gained a sense of mastering the stressor, and this strengthens her capacity to repeat this kind of activity again and in an effective way.

Similarly, when a director of Christian outreach (DCO) chooses a stressor, such as getting off the couch and onto the treadmill, his blood pressure may increase in preparation for the activity and during its performance. His body responds to the task at hand. Then, during the period of cooldown after the run, his heart rate and blood pressure return to normal. His body is ready to move on to the next activity. As with the deaconess, though, more has happened than just the exercise. In choosing this stressor and managing it, the DCO has increased his muscle tone, strength, and stamina. Exercise like this, repeated over time, will lower his resting heart rate and blood pressure, and will enhance his health in many other ways.

The development of healthy stress response patterns leads to greater personal capacity and to an increased sense of mastery. There is, however, a more negative pattern for processing stress. In this pattern, the person gets stuck in the first stage, the arousal or alarm stage. Over time, this can lead to chronic fatigue and, eventually, exhaustion.

When the preparation stage becomes chronic, when a sense of being in a conflict or danger persists, or when a battle, actual or perceived, is prolonged indefinitely, it exacts a serious price, both physically and emotionally. It's like starting a car, pressing the accelerator to the floor, and letting it run for days in a stationary position. Under those circumstances, the parts of the car will wear out more quickly than they would in normal use. Whether the threat is real or perceived, the effect is the same.

A recent study of church workers analyzed many health related issues (e.g., blood pressure, cholesterol levels, height, weight, exercise habits, age). The research also identified specific "stress events" each worker had experienced in the past year. Using statistical analysis, the researchers developed what they call a "Health Index" and a "Stress Index." This analysis showed

- A high correlation between perceived stress and the Health Index; if a worker agreed with the statement, "Stress has affected my health in the last year," that person's Health Index score was likely to be generally less positive overall.

- The higher the number of "stress events" the worker had experienced in the previous year, the lower the Health Index was likely to be.

- Workers who reported the most stress and the most stressor events in the past year also reported lower levels of satisfaction in multiple dimensions, including devotional life, vocational/job situation, and life in general.

- Even given these strong correlations, workers expressed little interest in changing stress management behaviors.[4]

Of course, correlations do not prove cause and effect. Even so, these results argue clearly and forcefully for a holistic approach to worker health in which all aspects of the worker's life is considered. Stressors abound for workers in the church. These workers often experience their stress as negative. Many are not managing their stress well. As a result, their bodies as well as their spirits deteriorate. As researchers learn more about the brain-body connection, they are concluding that psychology and biology work in tandem. There is no true separation.[5]

> Director of Christian education (DCE) Linda's resting blood pressure averages 150/95; her total cholesterol level is 245; her Body Mass Index (BMI) is 32, and she rarely takes time to exercise or to plan nutritional meals. Ten years ago, her resting blood pressure was 125/85, her total cholesterol level was 190, and her BMI was 28. On several fronts, the measures of Linda's Health Index are moving in a less healthy direction. Linda's doctor suggested a number of interventions, but Linda says, "I don't have time to do those things. I really can't slow down. The church is in a financial pinch, and if I don't do everything that is demanded—sorry, expected—of me, the church might decide it doesn't need me. I really need this job, and I really want to serve God's people. I guess I just have to keep running at this pace until . . . " At this point, Linda's voice trails off, leaving the sentence incomplete.

Like many church workers, Linda takes the host of demands and expectations of her congregation seriously. There are duties to perform, people to see, classes to teach, and meetings to attend. Like many workers, Linda chose church work because she wanted to serve Christ and His people. Being responsive to a host of people and their needs means living with a host of stressors. Therein lies one of the most significant vulnerabilities faced by church workers.

In some sense, such workers are like all the rest of us. Stressors fill all our lives; we all know what distress feels like. Expectations galore haunt the lives of most folks. But church workers are, at least in a human sense, beholden to those who pay their salaries, their parishioners. They are vulnerable to the demands and expectations of dozens and in some cases, hundreds of people. Additionally, they usually serve in the public light, the glare of which often increases their sense of vulnerability.

Research findings are clear: the more often an individual church worker experiences a chronic stress response, the less healthy that individual becomes. Conversely, the less healthy a church worker is, the more often he or she will experience less healthy recovery from the stress response.

SPEAKING PERSONALLY

The good news is that simply understanding stress can go a long way in helping human beings deal with it.[6] Yet many workers and their congregations haven't taken advantage of the remedies God, through science, provides. Perhaps this chapter (and this book) will help a bit.

In whatever capacity I have served in the church over the years, stressors and stress have been front-burner topics. Clients and co-workers alike have confronted issues of workload to time management. They have juggled the needs of spouse and family with pressures of getting work done. They have pitted the push for productivity against their personal need for self-care.

Stress-related disorders account for a significant number of work-related absences among the population in general, not just among church workers. I do see, however, that because of their vocation, many church workers experience more stressors than the average members to whom they minister. I also see that a worker's piety does not necessarily help him or her. We are taught to put ourselves second, and we are asked to respond to the needs of the others first. This is so even when we must sacrifice our health and, with it, our capacity to be responsive to the needs of others.

There is also the unsettling research that church workers seem less interested in learning about stress management. Likely this is where congregations can help.

I know that stressors in my own life play a major role in how I am feeling and how much energy I have to get tasks done. And I know that I am vulnerable to the temptation to fill my schedule to overflowing. I know that when I carry too many stressors, I grow inefficient and my productivity grinds to a slow crawl.

At one point, my wife and I moved into a home closer to work for both of us. I left the daily grind of rush hour traffic behind and in its place began a regular exercise routine. I also changed my eating habits. My resting blood pressure went down and I felt healthier. Had I more effectively managed my stress response? Perhaps.

We now turn to a deeper discussion of all this.

CHAPTER THREE

BURNOUT

"Wow, what a day," Carol thought to herself as she put her feet up and reached for the remote control. Reaching for the remote came much easier these days, though she still felt a twinge of guilt at spending so much time in mindless viewing. Feeling that twinge again, she put the remote down without turning on the television. "What is going on?" she wondered. "I've been teaching for six years now. I love the kids. But it's getting harder and harder to get up each morning to face the day. I'm feeling more and more tired and I'm not sleeping well. Maybe I'll talk to my principal. She might have some ideas about this," Carol mused.

Almost immediately, she had second thoughts. "No, that's not such a good idea. If she knows I'm struggling, she'll probably just tell me to get over it. She's under lots of stress herself, what with the financial predicament of the school and the tensions between her and the school board members. Besides, I don't want to ruin my reputation with her. Whatever made me want to teach in the first place?"

Carol stared out the window as she pondered the question. She thought about several caring teachers who had made such a difference in her own life. She thought about wanting to make that same kind of difference in the lives of other children. She thought about her excitement on the day when she walked into her classroom for the very first time. It had been the fulfillment of a dream. Other faculty members, her pastor, the members of the congregation had all seemed so warm and welcoming.

"I had energy, dreams, hopes—excitement!" Carol thought. "I can't remember a time when I felt more energized and more fulfilled than the first day of school that year. In many ways, my students were just like I had pictured them, and there I was, too, working with them, doing what I had always dreamed of doing."

Then a frown creased Carol's brow as her thoughts turned darker. She remembered early difficulties with discipline and conflicts with several parents over the years—mostly focused on a particular student's progress (or lack thereof). She thought about the increasing tensions between the church and school.

"Why does it always have to be about the money?" she asked herself. "The church and school are each barely able to balance their books, and the anxiety of it all flows right down to everyone on the staff. Worries about money lurk around every corner. None of us knows if we'll be teaching here next year or looking to move on because of staff layoffs. Even the kids' desks are falling apart because we can't afford to replace them."

As Carol thought about these things, she began to recognize that over the months and years she had become more inward-focused, keeping her feelings more and more to herself. "What's wrong with me!?" she asked, half-afraid to face the answer. "Should I be doing something else with my life? Is God using my unhappiness to point me in a different direction? Am I depressed? Maybe there's something wrong with my faith. I should be able to shake this off. But I can't. I need to do something about this downward spiral. But what? Quit teaching? Talk to a friend? Find a counselor? Pray more?"

Someone has said that in order to burn out, a person must once have been on fire. Carol was once "on fire" for teaching. Now, that blaze has turned to embers, and Carol has begun to see herself as burned out. You're not a likely candidate for burnout if you entered church work

- with limited passion to serve others or make a difference in their lives.
- because you thought it would put you in a position of power or prestige.
- hoping to earn a maximum amount of money for a minimum of effort.
- because you found the potential for vacation time and holidays inviting.

On the other hand, church workers are more likely candidates for burnout if they bring to the task a passion for

- sharing the Gospel of Jesus Christ.
- fulfilling the calling the Holy Spirit has given them.
- helping deepen people's relationship with the triune God.
- walking closely with the people they love, sharing both burdens and joys.

Church workers share their vulnerability to burnout with all people of passion who have chosen service-oriented vocations. Experts have studied and defined burnout for several decades. We hear the term bandied about in the media and in everyday conversation between friends. It's helpful to consider the specific characteristics experts have developed over the years. What is burnout?

Most experts think of it in terms of a progressive loss of energy, of idealism and purpose. Those in the helping professions are especially vulnerable to it, especially when they find themselves facing challenges for which they have not been adequately trained. Task overload, too many hours at work, and low pay contribute to burnout, as do bureaucratic or political constraints. All these conditions lead to a gap between what the person aspires to accomplish and what can actually be done.[1]

Burnout manifests itself in specific physical symptoms—difficulty sleeping, weight loss or gain, headaches, gastrointestinal disturbances, low-grade depression, a nagging boredom, and chronic tiredness that doesn't go away after a good night's sleep or a few days of vacation.[2]

In short, burnout is the exhaustion brought about by a loss of idealism resulting from the conditions in which one works. Emotional, physical, mental, and even spiritual exhaustion are its central features. The worker feels helpless, hopeless, and trapped. In addition, workers suffering from burnout develop negative attitudes about themselves, their work, and life itself. They often have trouble praying and reading the Scriptures. They may doubt Christ's presence. It is easy to see these characteristics in Carol, the teacher described in this chapter's opening vignette.

Burnout poses a clear occupational hazard for anyone whose basic identity involves service to others, especially in a context of idealism and mission. Church workers are especially vulnerable because most of them have a high sense of mission, of wanting to serve others. In general, they want to make a difference in the lives of others and in the world, and they carry a strong sense of duty to their vocation and a desire to live up to the ideals of the Church for whom Jesus Christ died.

These are all positive characteristics. However, the commitment to mission must be lived out in the real world, a world broken by sin. In that world, no one can effectively engage in mission all the time, nor can church workers serve successfully in every situation, or make a difference in the lives of every person to whom they min-

LIFE IN THE REAL CHURCH ON EARTH DIFFERS FROM LIFE IN THE IDEAL CHURCH.

ister. Nor will they obey Christ perfectly in every circumstance. Life in the real church on earth differs from life
in the ideal Church, and because of it, burnout can and
often does occur. It is tempting to blame the person who
is experiencing burnout, but to do so ignores reality. To
do so denies that conditions, contexts, and circumstances
sometimes come together to maximize the worker's vulnerability to burnout—especially in the lives of some of
the Church's best and most empathic workers. If not for
the passion, the idealism, the commitment to serve others,
and zeal for the Gospel of Jesus Christ, vulnerability to
burnout would diminish. But because churches and schools
expect, support, encourage, and even demand these characteristics, burnout is an ever-present danger.

In short, the better a worker exemplifies the qualities and behaviors congregations see as exceptional, the
more vulnerable they are to burnout. This is so because
our ideals bump up against the realities of a broken, sinful
world. In an ideal world, every member of the congregation would work in harmony for the cause of Christ. In
the real world, congregations often experience significant
conflicts. Sometimes even whole denominations struggle
with serious infighting and political intrigue. People who
enter their vocation motivated by high ideals eventually
need to deal with the reality that ideals are often lived out
imperfectly, regardless of what is preached and taught.

Think back to Carol, the teacher whose story began
this chapter. In an ideal world, Carol would teach every
lesson in ways that interest and engage her students. She
would make a difference in her students' lives every day in

the same way she remembers her own teachers doing that. In an ideal world, every student would learn eagerly—just as Carol remembers herself doing.

In the real world, though, Carol struggles with effectiveness. She has discovered that not all students are eager learners. Carol's idealism and a desire to serve propelled her into teaching; those same qualities, bumping up against reality, are instigating her burnout.

In an ideal situation, every faculty member in Carol's school would get along famously. Conflict would be minimal. The principal would be safe and approachable, empathic and helpful. The real-world situation, in contrast, includes conflicts between teachers, conflicts between teachers and the principal, conflicts between leaders of the school and church. In the real world, Carol's principal seems less than approachable.

In an ideal world, Carol would receive an excellent wage. She would find herself valued and supported by the parents because of her work with her students. In the real world, though, Carol's compensation is barely adequate, the school board has just lowered the school's subsidy for the staff health insurance plan, and several parents have expressed unhappiness with Carol's instructional approach.

At many turns, Carol's idealism has been challenged, her enthusiasm dampened by encounters with the realities of a less than ideal situation. Feeling unsupported and increasingly lonely, Carol has turned to television for a more or less mindless way to fill up her time. She has turned more and more into herself, and she has become increasingly disconsolate, depressed, and, to use the central theme of this discussion, burned out.

While burnout has the potential to affect many of us, the most vulnerable are people like Carol—people with a deep sense of mission, a passionate desire to give of themselves in and to the service of others, and people who have set a very high bar for themselves. The deeper the sense of mission, the more the vulnerability to burnout; the greater the passion to serve, the deeper the vulnerability to burnout.

The very characteristics the church most wants in those who serve are the characteristics that set the stage for burnout. Thus, congregations do bear considerable responsibility for preventing burnout and for managing those things that set the stage for it in the first place.

SPEAKING PERSONALLY

I tend to see myself as a person who wants to be in relationships with others, and I want those relationships to be useful and helpful. I do not always do that as well as I could or should. At times, I most certainly fall short and flee to Jesus Christ with my shortcomings. At times, I end up caring more about myself, about my own needs, desires, wants, and ambitions than I do about serving others. When I become aware of it, I flee to Jesus Christ. The amazing thing is that He surrounds me with His love, forgives me where I have been self-serving instead of other-serving, and empowers me through His Holy Spirit for serving His people in healthy ways.

Because service to others is a major motivating force

in my life and in my identity, I am vulnerable to burnout. Truth be told, I find it difficult to say no when I see a human need in front of me. The danger in this is that I will serve and serve and serve, go and go and go, until I am exhausted.

One cannot run a race indefinitely.

I have experienced burnout. I know its face. I know that I am vulnerable to it. I know what it feels like. So when I speak of burnout, I speak both from the standpoint of professional analysis and from that of personal experience. I also speak of it having witnessed so many church workers exhausting themselves and having witnessed many congregations encouraging such behavior in the name of Christ. This causes me real pain, for if it continues, I know it will propel even more workers into unhealthy behaviors and, finally, into burnout.

CHAPTER FOUR

SECONDARY TRAUMATIC STRESS

A pastor for twenty-three years, Micah took a deep breath as he entered his office following the funeral and graveside rites for a young child killed in a house fire. "Trapped in an upstairs bedroom," he muttered. "What a waste!" Micah was shaking. He felt his heart pounding. He knew his face was red. He slammed his fist on his desk, winced at the pain, slumped in his chair, and began to sob.

Micah was no slouch in the pastoral office. Now in his second parish, Micah knew members respected him. They especially treasured the pastoral care he gave in times of significant trouble, illness, stress, or transitions. He had a reputation for helping as quickly as possible whenever he heard about a crisis in the life of one of his members. He also served actively in a local community rape crisis center and had helped several of its clients connect to the parish.

After awhile, Micah composed himself, at least somewhat. He offered a heartfelt prayer, asking Christ for comfort and for His continuing presence. Then he left the office and went home. As he walked in the back door, he kissed his wife and waved to his two adolescent children in the family room. "I'm tired," he said. "I'm going to take a nap."

He was up by dinnertime. Still, he continued to feel what he later came to call "shell shock." He was noticeably withdrawn and reserved. "Something got you down, Dad?" his daughter asked. "Just a tough day," Micah responded, and put some food into his mouth. That ended the conversation in that direction.

In the days that followed, Micah walked through his duties and obligations, but the spark that others were used to seeing in his eyes had dimmed considerably. Both his administrative assistant and his spouse asked about this. But somehow Micah did not want to pursue it with them. "Maybe," he thought to himself, "this is just something that I have to suck up. God will carry me through it."

Over the next few weeks, a few members and the director of the rape crisis clinic asked, "Is anything wrong, Pastor?" He responded in the same way to each—it was "just a taxing time in ministry." While true enough, the words and Micah's body language clearly said, "Leave me alone." It worked, ending further conversation.

Still, Micah sensed that something was truly off-kilter. Finally, he phoned a close friend, another pastor in the community.

The two met in the friend's office, and after an exchange of pleasantries, Micah began. "I just feel dead inside," he said. "I remember the first months of my ministry. I felt alive! I was eager to make evangelism and hospital calls. Visiting with shut-ins was a joy. I relished witnessing to the resurrection of Christ and offering the hope of the resurrection to dying parishioners and to their families at their funerals."

"But now . . ." His voice trailed off. After a moment, he continued, "But now I dread all the things I used to love. I'm doing what I need to do, but I have little life left and no energy to put into them."

Micah's friend had seen Micah as others had, as a marvelous and well-connected-to-his-parishioners pastor. Over the years, Micah had gained a well-deserved reputation of responsiveness to the spiritual, emotional, and even physical needs of those he served. Faithful. Dedicated. Energetic. Christocentric. Micah's peers and parishioners alike would use these words to describe him. But little by little Micah's zeal and energy had diminished.

Taking a deep breath with tears welling up in his eyes, Micah asked, "What in the world has happened to me? What is happening to me?"

What *is* happening to Pastor Micah? Early in his ministerial career, Pastor Micah walked alongside a person who was dying and then conducted his first funeral. The

92-year-old woman left behind three grieving children, seven grieving grandchildren, two grieving great-grand-children, and a grieving younger sister. Emotions ran high. Greatly loved by her family, the deceased was widely admired by members of her congregation. On a hypothetical trauma-level scale of 1–10, those involved experienced this woman's death at different levels. Her sister experienced it at a level 8, her children at a level 9, her grandchildren at a level 6, and her great-grandchildren as a level 4. Pastor Micah, though not a family member, also felt a sense of loss. He had connected empathically to members of the family. His experience of this death on our hypothetical scale was .75—a little less than level 1. He ministered to the individuals; he was not involved in the same direct sense the family members were.

In the great scheme of things, .75 is not a lot of trauma, but it is some trauma. In the first five years of his ministry, Pastor Micah accompanied seven people through the death process. He conducted all seven of their funerals and two more besides. If each of these inflicted an average trauma-scale rating of .75, the trauma impact he absorbed in those first five years added up to 6.75.

Additionally, Pastor Micah had rushed to the emergency room four times over those five years to minister to parishioners suffering from chest pains. All had suffered heart attacks, all recovered, and all cite their time in the emergency room as a very frightening experience. On our hypothetical trauma scale, they each reached a level 4; Pastor Micah experienced each at a level of .25. If we add that into his previous cumulative trauma score, we see that score now stands at 7.75.

The parents of the child who died in the house fire experienced the child's death at a trauma level 10. Pastor Micah's experience of this death was at least a level 3. Even if Pastor Micah had experienced no other trauma in the intervening years, the child's death has raised his cumulative trauma score beyond our maximum hypothetical number.

If Pastor Micah were more detached from his work and from the people whom he serves, if he were content to spend most of his time in his office in sermon preparation and chatting with other clergy on the Internet, if he were to see his vocation in a more mechanical and distant way, he would be less vulnerable to what has happened to him. But he is not. He is, or at least he has been, the kind of pastor most folks want. But he is paying a personal price.

Recently, clinicians and researchers have begun to study in depth a concept they call "Secondary Traumatic Stress." They have discovered that a person does not have to be personally involved in a trauma to be affected by it; the person simply needs to be available to the emotional state of those who are directly involved.

There is often a fine line between direct traumatic stress and its secondary forms. A pastor present at the suicide of a young man and also providing pastoral care to the young man's parents will experience the trauma directly and will also be affected by its secondary manifestations. Likewise, Pastor Micah, who was there when his 92-year-old parishioner took her last breaths and who also provided pastoral care to her sister, children, grandchildren, and great-grandchildren, experienced the trauma directly and also experienced its secondary manifestations.

Pastor Micah was not directly involved at the fire scene, nor was he present when firefighters recovered the body of the child. But as he gave pastoral care to the grieving parents and as he conducted the funeral service, he most certainly experienced Secondary Traumatic Stress.

The experiences of returning military veterans have helped to make that more evident. As psychologists have learned more about how to treat the posttraumatic stress of veterans, more of those veterans have sought help. As that has happened, the psychiatrists, psychologists, military chaplains, and other professionals who serve these veterans have often found themselves in need of support. As a result, Secondary Traumatic Stress has gained increasingly wide recognition as a genuine condition. Helping professionals themselves often need help. Just as we offer direct and intentional care to the first responders in automobile accidents and airliner crashes, so, too, we need to make direct and intentional care available to those who serve as first responders in emotional trauma. Recent research tells us that such support is important for the health and well-being of those who work with people.

Later in the conversation with his friend, Pastor Micah mused, "Maybe keeping all this stuff inside of me has taken its toll." He's probably right!

Every teacher, director of Christian education, director of Christian outreach, deaconess, and pastor will be affected by Secondary Traumatic Stress to some degree. Those who connect most deeply, compassionately, empathically, and caringly with people during difficult times will be affected most. The effect is cumulative and, eventually, it can damage the capacity of church workers to perform their duties.

The formula is relatively straightforward and simple: the more deeply a caregiver opens himself or herself up to the thoughts and feelings of others, the more vulnerable the caregiver will be to "catching" those thoughts and feelings. The deeper the struggle, pain, hurt, and grief the hurting person experiences, the deeper the effect will be in the caregiver. There is a direct relationship here. The deeper the care given, the more vulnerable the caregiver becomes.

Another formula is at work too. Pastor Micah expresses it when he wonders, "Maybe keeping all this stuff inside of me has taken its toll." The more church workers keep what is happening to them caged up inside themselves, the more vulnerable they become and the more likely it is that their experiences will have a toxic affect.

Pastor Micah's members want him to care for them in a deep and empathetic way. Most parishioners want this capacity in all their workers. Most parishioners, for example, want their pastor to visit them in the hospital when they are ill. They want their pastor to listen to their emotions, to share their hopes, and to take their needs to the throne of grace in fervent prayer. That is what Pastor Micah did—and he is paying a steep spiritual and emotional price for doing so. Over time, he has found himself caught up in all the emotions that have been part of his experiences with his parishioners. He has "caught" their traumas, and the cumulative experiences have finally caught up with him.

Pastor Micah's own personal style and the expectations of his congregation have made him vulnerable. His congregation gladly receives his care, but they are not as attuned as they need to be in how to care for him.

SPEAKING PERSONALLY

Have you ever talked with church workers who have "retired" emotionally while still serving actively? I have. I believe that Secondary Traumatic Stress is one of the primary causes. It's not good for the worker or for those served. And it doesn't have to be this way!

Have you ever talked with church workers who, early in their careers, were excited go-getters but who now somehow have lost that energy, that spark? I have. I believe that Secondary Traumatic Stress is one of the primary causes. It's not good for the institutions those workers serve. It doesn't have to be this way!

Have you ever talked with church workers who, early in their careers, were excited go-getters and who somehow have retained that energy and that spark even though they will retire in a few months? I have. These are the workers who have learned to deal with Secondary Traumatic Stress. It can and should be this way in the Body of Christ.

Have you ever talked with someone new to church work, someone full of enthusiasm, passion, and energy, someone who really wants to change the world? Have you wondered if that spark, that energy, will survive ten, twenty, or thirty years? I have, and I know that, at least from a human perspective, the answer to my question will depend in large part on whether or not the worker learns to attend to Secondary Traumatic Stress.

I believe this is a crucial factor in church worker health, one that both workers and parishioners have neglected. Other people-serving professions have begun to attend to it. I think it is time that we in the church do too.

I have invested most of my career in direct service to people. As a pastoral counselor, I've helped shape programs in support of the health and wellness of church workers, their spouses, and their families. In recent years, I've helped shape the attitudes and understandings of future pastors and deaconesses. I encourage them continually to immerse themselves in God's grace through Word and Sacrament. I urge them to call on other members of the Body of Christ for support, admonition, and encouragement. I believe with all my heart that the best additional advice I can give is to them is this:

Don't keep everything inside. Get your emotional reactions from the inside to the outside. In Baptism, we are brought into a new relationship with God and into new relationships with each other. God has put us together for mutual support. Use it!

GOD HAS PUT US TOGETHER FOR MUTUAL SUPPORT.

THE RESOURCES
CHRIST GIVES

The vulnerabilities church workers face are significant. The characteristics and behaviors most congregations want in their workers are the very things that can become most problematic for those workers. Satan and his forces oppose workers who prayerfully and faithfully wrestle to connect the truths of God's Word with the experiences of those they serve. Workers who hold high ideals and hopes for themselves and their church or school will be forced to face the realities of imperfect people and imperfect organizations. High hopes, expectations, and vision often collide with the realities of human sin. This clash makes church workers vulnerable to burnout.

The vulnerability only increases when workers come to their tasks with zeal, energy, compassion, and care and as they minister in difficult and emotionally charged situations. Walking closely beside people with significant problems and emotional traumas can leave the worker open to secondary traumatic stress and its consequences.

What's more, the more effective the worker's service, the more the dangers grow—spiritually, physically, and emotionally.

How can the Christian community respond to these challenges?

In this section, I will examine a few over-arching principles of life together in the Christian community, principles that support the health, well-being, and spiritual hardiness of workers and those they serve. We begin with the bigger picture of attitudes and "ways of being" in the congregation, because when the community of faith is less than fully healthy, any specific suggestions I can give about worker support will be less than fully effective.

A congregation's way of being the Body of Christ with and for one another is crucial. How does the church do business? How does it foster healthy interaction between members? How does it support Christlike behaviors? How does it foster health-enhancing care, mission, and ministry?

The very best support church workers can receive is the opportunity to serve in settings that are essentially healthy. Random acts of support by individuals and groups make a difference, of course. Occasional retreats and getaways are important, but often have short-lived affects. Organizational health and well-being are central and more enduringly health-enhancing for the church worker. When the organization dynamics and behaviors are positive and healthy, based in authentic relationships, and formed and nourished by Word and Sacrament, they deliver the best kind of support a church worker can receive. When the organization is as healthy as possible, given our fallen world and the sinful nature of every member, then creative, specific, supportive actions will spontaneously follow.

As God's people gather around Word and Sacrament, they do so as the community of the baptized. Everyone who is baptized into Christ has put on Christ. We are members of His Body. Our broken relationship with God has been mended in the cross, and we now enjoy restored relationships with the other members of Christ's Body. Christ brings rich resources into our midst. This identity is basic to all we do.

The community of the baptized has the potential for positive life together as we live it at the foot of the cross and in the power of the empty tomb. Led by the Holy Spirit, members of our community live in forgiveness, appreciation, health, and well-being, despite the fallenness of the world around us.

This then leads to two overall suggestions concerning life together in support of church workers:

1. The creation of a Worker Support Team (WST).

2. The use of behavioral covenants to guide relationships and expectations between parishioners and their workers.

Both of these suggestions, embedded in the understanding of the local congregation or school as the Body of Christ, will give rise to specific strategies helpful to church workers as they deal with the vulnerabilities described in Section 1.

CHAPTER FIVE

LIFE TOGETHER AS CHRIST'S BODY

All church workers serve in a context—in individual congregations, institutions, or schools. These organizations can be health-enhancing. Or they can be places about which members and workers say, "It makes me sick."

Organizational health is central to the health of the members of the organization. It is no different with congregations and schools. Thus, when we want to support church workers, we begin by focusing on organizational health. St. Paul gives this significant emphasis in his writings. In Ephesians 4, 1 Corinthians 12–13, and Romans 12, the apostle paints a magnificent picture of the Christian community. Together, the community of believers forms the Body of Christ, in relationship with one another because of Christ's work for us.

These relationships are not simply human bonds, forged by the convergence of human needs. Christ Himself has created them; He sustains them. These relationships are His gift to us.

> Ever since Jill had worked on the annual spaghetti dinner with Anne, she felt irritated every time Anne came into view. "Anne really likes to have her own way," Jill thought, "She just rubs me the

wrong way. If she would just ramp down some of her pushiness, maybe I could at least stand her."

During their evening devotions together one night, Jill and her husband, Steve, happened upon 1 Corinthians 12. Two verses caught Jill's heart and mind: "For in one Spirit we were all baptized into one body—Jews or Greeks, slaves or free—and all were made to drink of one Spirit" (1 Corinthians 12:13) and "But as it is, God arranged the members in the body, each one of them, as He chose" (1 Corinthians 12:18).

"I am very convicted by these passages," Jill said softly. "I have let my irritation with Anne cloud the bond that Christ has given us. I have seen her as pushy, as Anne-the-Irritant rather than as a person God has placed with me in the Body of Christ. I wonder what God is teaching me?"

Jill had no easy answers to this new question, at least not yet. But the Word had grabbed Jill's attention. Steve and Jill closed their devotions together in prayer, and Jill resolved to discuss this emerging spiritual issue with Deaconess Shirley in the next day or so.

That people in the Christian community differ from one another is self-evident. It's underscored by all the "body language" Paul uses. But Paul also makes it clear that despite our differences, every part of the Body belongs and is held together in, through, and by Christ. Consider:

> Rather, speaking the truth in love, we are to grow up in every way into Him who is the head,

into Christ, from whom the whole body, joined
and held together by every joint with which it is
equipped, when each part is working properly,
makes the body grow so that it builds itself up in
love. (Ephesians 4:15–16)

Now there are varieties of gifts, but the same Spirit; and there are varieties of service, but the same
Lord; and there are varieties of activities, but it is
the same God who empowers them all in everyone. To each is given the manifestation of the Spirit for the common good. (1 Corinthians 12:4–7)

For as in one body we have many members, and
the members do not all have the same function,
so we, though many, are one body in Christ, and
individually members one of another. (Romans
12:4–5)

We are connected to one another in the Christian
community not simply by the bonds of human relationships and good will, not simply by the bonds of emotion
and personal experience, but fundamentally, we are joined
together in and through Christ. We celebrate the gifts
Christ gives each of us for the good of all of us, and we work
to help one another enhance and grow the gifts Christ has
given. We want to see the Body grow as it "builds itself up
love" (Ephesians 4:16).

Christ calls us to this. Paul writes, "I therefore, a pris-
oner for the Lord, urge you to walk in a manner worthy
of the calling to which you have been called" (Ephesians
4:1). Because the community exists by virtue of Jesus

Christ, the community is marked by certain behavioral and ethical characteristics. Paul identifies some of these in Ephesians 4:25–32.

- **TELL THE TRUTH.** This is key. It includes not lying to or about one another. It also includes telling the whole truth rather than partial-truths. Paul encourages us, "Therefore, having put away falsehood, let each one of you speak the truth with his neighbor, for we are members one of another" (Ephesians 4:25). Paul grounds this first ethic in God's grace, in the reality that Christ has made us members with one another.

- **DO NOT LET EMOTION CAUSE DIVISION.** Strong emotions can drive wedges between people. Satan lurks, ready to exploit this truth. That's one reason Paul writes, "Be angry and do not sin; do not let the sun go down on your anger, and give no opportunity to the devil" (Ephesians 4:26–27). People will have emotional responses to one another's words and actions. Apparently, the emotion is not the problem; how we deal with our emotions can be. As Christ's baptized people, we want to use emotion in constructive ways to build up the Body. We address conflicts that arise; we don't allow them to simmer and grow. This is part of the spiritual warfare God calls us to engage.

- **WORK.** Among other things, work has a utilitarian purpose in the Body: it provides resources we can give to those in need. Again, Paul writes, "Let the thief no longer steal, but rather let him labor, doing honest work with his own hands, so that he may have something to share with anyone in need" (Ephesians 4:28). We work for ourselves, but we also work for the sake of others.

- **SPEAK GRACIOUSLY.** We intend that our words build up others in Christ's Body. We want what we say to nourish, sustain, and support others. Destructive speech has no place in the Body. "Let no corrupting talk come out of your mouths, but only such as is good for building up, as fits the occasion, that it may give grace to those who hear" (Ephesians 4:29).

- **REMEMBER YOUR BAPTISM.** In Baptism, Christ has sealed us as His own. Our redemption is secure. Even so, we can sadden the Spirit of God by our words and actions. Indeed, the Spirit may weep over our behaviors. Paul writes, "Do not grieve the Holy Spirit of God, by whom you were sealed for the day of redemption" (Ephesians 4:30). Our baptismal seal comforts us, even as it calls us to new ways of being and doing. Though we sometimes fail, Christ's cross is ever before us, sustaining us.

- **GET RID OF THE NEGATIVE AND DESTRUCTIVE STUFF!** "Let all bitterness and wrath and anger and clamor and slander be put away from you, along with all malice" (Ephesians 4:31). Paul's language includes no ambiguity. The term he uses, "be put away," is very strong.

■ **LIVE OUT THE CHRISTLIKE ATTITUDES AND BEHAVIORS OF YOUR NEW IDENTITY!** "Be kind to one another, tenderhearted, forgiving one another, as God in Christ forgave you" (Ephesians 4:32). Once again, St. Paul returns to his central, foundational theme: Christ has forgiven us; Christ propels us into relationship with others. Those relationships take as their template Christ's own behaviors. We emulate His example by His grace.

■ **LOVE.** When you get right down to it, the core issue is love—love made possible by the love Christ first showed us, love animated by our membership in the Body of Christ. Everything comes from Christ. Paul writes, "Be imitators of God, as beloved children. And walk in love, as Christ loved us and gave Himself up for us, a fragrant offering and sacrifice to God" (Ephesians 5:1–2). There is no genuine community without Christ, who gave Himself into death for us and who holds all things together.

Paul created a similar list in Romans 12. In addition to the behaviors listed in Ephesians 4, the apostle includes these in Romans 12:

■ **SHARE FEELINGS LIBERALLY WITH OTHERS.** This includes feelings both of a positive and negative variety. "Rejoice with those who rejoice, weep with those who weep," the text tells us (Romans 12:15). This sharing of feelings would seem to point to the capacity of people to empathize with one another and to help one another more deeply understand experiences.

- **AVOID VENGEFUL THOUGHTS AND BEHAV-IORS.** Instead, look for the good. "Repay no one evil for evil, but give thought to do what is honorable in the sight of all" (Romans 12:17). We focus on the positive and on doing positive things, even in the midst of evil behaviors by others.

- **MAKE IT YOUR AIM TO DO GOOD.** As God's baptized children, we need not let evil overwhelm us. The apostle counsels, "Do not be overcome by evil, but overcome evil with good" (Romans 12:21). These words sound a note of hopefulness. Christ was victorious over sin, death, and the devil. As we cling to our Savior, evil cannot overcome us.

Paul paints a clear picture of the Christian Community. Christ creates the Body, and He is its core and center. Diversely and abundantly gifted, this Body builds itself up in love as the Spirit strengthens it. Claimed by Christ, members of His Body fulfill certain ethical standards, imperatives, and expectations as we relate to one another and as we interact with those outside the fellowship. Ephesians 4 and 1 Corinthians 12 both point to our central motivation—love.

> Jill had a lot on her mind when she met with Deaconess Shirley. Her anger and irritation at Anne had turned inward. Now she was unhappy with herself. "I ought to be dealing with this in a different way," she lamented to Deaconess Shirley. As they talked, the way seemed clear: Jill would need to talk directly with Anne. Deacon-

ess Shirley reminded Jill of the forgiveness that Jill had received in the work of Christ. She and Jill prayed together. The next day Jill called Anne and invited her out for tea.

The conversation went well. Jill explained she had been reacting to Anne's behavior and asked for forgiveness. Anne recognized that her assertiveness had been a problem for Jill. Anne asked Jill for forgiveness for her insensitivity. Together the two women rejoiced that their relationship had been repaired and for the presence of Jesus Christ in their midst. Most certainly Christ was present in their conversation, for that was and is His promise.

In words and actions, Jill and Anne lived out the description of the Body in the letter James wrote to the Early Church:

> Is anyone among you suffering? Let him pray. Is anyone cheerful? Let him sing praise. Is anyone among you sick? Let him call for the elders of the church, and let them pray over him, anointing him with oil in the name of the Lord. And the prayer of faith will save the one who is sick, and the Lord will raise him up. And if he has committed sins, he will be forgiven. Therefore, confess your sins to one another and pray for one another, that you may be healed. The prayer of a righteous person has great power as it is working. (James 5:13–16)

Like everything in the Church, our support for the workers God sends to us grows out of our identity as the community created by Christ, His Body. We respect one another, and we treasure the diverse gifts our Lord has given each member. We use our gifts to build up the Body, and we follow the ethical and behavioral imperatives God has given, imperatives that are necessary for the Body to flourish.

SPEAKING PERSONALLY

When we join forces in organizations, we often can accomplish much more than we ever could as individuals. But organizational dynamics can wear people down instead of building them up; those dynamics can help members stay healthy or help sicken them. You've probably seen and perhaps even experienced this. I know I have.

I have also worked through a number of exercises and workshops designed to promote organizational health. Many books have this as their theme. I've referenced some of them in the "Additional Resources" section at the end of the book.

Still, if I do not begin and end with Christ, my work with organizations is neither churchly nor, in the most holistic sense, healthy. I used to think that if we opened and closed with prayer, asking the Holy Spirit to guide us, that that would ensure success. I ignored one key and often missing ingredient—my own responsibility and willingness to hold myself and others accountable for healthy, Christlike behaviors.

The most faith-challenging experiences of my life have come as I have observed the inner workings of congregations and church organizations. At times, what I have seen has shocked me. I've watched as leaders allowed, condoned, or even supported uncivil behaviors—all under the guise of piety and righteousness. Only the content of the conversation seemed to matter. No one challenged or even discussed behavior. The Pauline emphasis on behavioral ethics that follow from membership in the Body of Christ was somehow lost.

In writing this, I am painfully aware of my own shortcomings in this regard. The imperatives Paul sets before us in Ephesians, Romans, and 1 Corinthians make it clear that I fall dramatically and radically short of the ideal. The picture Paul paints differs drastically from my own sinful words and deeds. Recognizing this reality, I flee for refuge to Christ's cross.

Yet, assured of His forgiveness, those ethical imperatives beckon me to a healthier life, as they beckon all humankind. They call all congregations toward becoming healthier organizations. They offer hope, the hope that flows from the truth that the Body of Christ is centered in Christ and enabled by Him to become more like Him.

All of this helps me live in optimism and hope that our congregations, institutions, and schools can become more and more places where St. Paul's words ring true:

> Therefore be imitators of God, as beloved children. And walk in love, as Christ loved us and gave Himself up for us, a fragrant offering and sacrifice to God. (Ephesians 5:1–2)

CHAPTER SIX

COMMUNITIES OF AUTHENTIC ENCOUNTER AND APPRECIATION

© 2011 Baloocartoon.com

"When do you see your boss?" Ken Blanchard of *One Minute Manager* fame once asked a group of industrial workers. Many replied, "When I've done something wrong." Blanchard suggests that a supervisor's more appropriate role is to "catch" people doing things well in order to recognize and support both the behavior and the workers' positive sense of themselves.

It's not a new concept. Millennia ago, the Wisdom Literature of the Old Testament told God's people: "The light of the eyes rejoices the heart, and good news refreshes the bones" (Proverbs 15:30). Moreover, "Gracious words are like a honeycomb, sweetness to the soul and health to the body" (Proverbs 16:24).

Few would doubt that words of kindness, understanding, appreciation, and praise uplift the human spirit. Words like that may even have a positive effect on one's physical health. In contrast, words that malign, distort, diminish, and criticize tear people down. Most certainly, "Death and life are in the power of the tongue" (Proverbs 18:21).

What would happen if the members of a congregation, as a part of its essential culture, intentionally noticed and affirmed others doing good things? Similarly, what would happen if members identified its strengths and rejoiced in them, and then worked to build on those strengths?

SCENE 1:

Sheila, the director of Christian education at St. James' Church, sat at her desk, preparing a devotional thought for the youth group leadership team scheduled to meet in ten minutes. In popped Sam, a member of that team, followed by his parents. Sam's dad spoke first. "Hi, Sheila! Sam's mom and I have been talking about the youth program here. We think it has really moved forward under your leadership. We so appreciate your creativity and the careful way you plan the projects for the kids. Plus, you follow through really well. If Sam is any indication, the kids like you and trust you. We brought you this card. It repeats what I just said." Sam's mom broke in, "I agree. Thanks, Sheila. We really appreciate your work." A broad smile came to Sam Junior's face.

Sheila's face lit up, too, as she replied, "Thanks for the feedback, I really appreciate it. And I'd like to add that it's a great joy to work with Sam. He is a gifted young man, full of energy and always ready to lend a hand to others. The other day I noticed him talking with one of the other members of the leadership team. From a distance, it looked like Sam offered to pray with him, and they did. Sam, you've got a heart for people!"

By this time Sam was beaming. As the family left, Sheila sat back in her chair, feeling a warm glow in her heart.

....

SCENE 2:

Al, now in his second year of teaching at St. James' Church, walked into his eighth grade classroom half an hour before the school doors opened. His principal, Audrey, with whom he had developed a great relationship, greeted him. She had worked hard to help Al integrate into the school faculty, made herself available to him as he struggled through a couple of behavioral issues with his students, and hosted him, along with the rest of the faculty, at her home a couple of times each year.

"I just wanted you to know," said Audrey, "that I think your work with the students around this year's special mission project has been outstanding. The students seemed to have responded really well, and I got a call from one of the parents last night saying she has never seen her child so interested in anything that has to do with mission work. Way to go!"

Al smiled and said, "Thanks."

Al was raised simply to do his duty, to accomplish what was expected of him. As a youngster, he had dreamed about teaching some day, much like his own seventh grade teacher. Al's family expected excellence but rarely commented on it. On the other hand, if Al failed to perform with excellence, he was sure to hear about it from his dad. In fact, when Audrey complimented him, Al thought, "This is so weird. I'm just doing what I was trained to do, what I'm supposed to do. I suppose I'm doing it well. I'm not looking for some kind of reward for that! So what's the big deal?"

As Audrey left, Al sat down in his chair and sighed deeply, a contented kind of sigh. "It is good to know that I am appreciated," Al thought to himself. "Praise be to God that I am able to do well what I am called to do."

The words of affirmation in both these interactions made a difference because they grew out of ongoing relationships. Because these relationships had been cultivated over months and years, the words carried more weight. Spoken in a context of transparency and authenticity, the affirmation meant a lot.

What would happen if a congregation encouraged its members to develop significant relationships with one another? What if those relationships grew deep and the congregation became a place of authentic personal encounter, with God in Word and Sacrament and with one another, the members of the Body of Christ? Person-to-person relationships create a context in which words of appreciation can be spoken and received as meaningful and truthful. To show true caring for one another requires that members feel safe in making their needs known. It also requires that those who hear about an individual's need have the desire and the capacity to respond in understanding, practical, and empathic ways.

Many observers have pointed out that a major problem of the church in North America today is that the people who gather together as members have few authentic encounters with one another. Often, the emphasis lies on how a person looks on the outside rather than on engaging one another authentically, on supporting one another during real-life challenges.

In order to carry out this pretense, people must follow rules like these: don't talk, don't feel, don't trust, and don't want. To fit in, people must appear good, pious, and happy when they come to church regardless of what they are actually feeling on the inside. For someone struggling with an addiction to pornography, for instance, "don't want" means the person must not want to change or believe that change is possible. Such people are pressured to shut down their feelings about what is happening and resign themselves to what they consider inevitable. They isolate themselves because they cannot trust others with the knowledge of their struggle.

Plug any problem or concern into this formula. The unwritten rule says that those with problems must keep the problems to themselves. No one else in the Christian community can know. After all, what would "they" think? Is someone feeling depressed? She should keep it to herself because Christians are supposed to be joyful. Is someone having marital problems? He should keep it to himself, because Christian marriages should be textbook perfect. Rather than fostering genuine Christian community, the church becomes a place of pretense.

In contrast, communities of authentic encounter foster genuine and transparent communications. People share what is going on in their lives and then come together in prayer, care, and mutual support. Communities like this enact what the Lutheran Confessions call the "mutual conversation and consolation of brethren" (Smalcald Articles III IV 1).

....

SCENE 3:

Jane had not been feeling well for some time. It wasn't just the aches and pains of her aging, now 71-year-old body. It was the awareness that she was becoming more forgetful. At least, she thought so. It wasn't so much big things. She hadn't forgotten to lock the house when she left. She hadn't driven some place and then been unable to find her way home. But some smaller things worried her. She sometimes forgot to return phone calls. She missed appointments she had failed to write down. Sometimes she just couldn't come up with the right word, at least not as quickly as she wanted. And she sometimes lost her train of thought. "Better to face this directly," Jane thought, and she made an appointment with her doctor. After listening to her symptoms, her doctor recommended an MRI brain scan.

Jane took special care on Sunday morning to be "put together" well. She applied her makeup carefully and dressed her best. When she walked into church, she felt worried on the inside, but worked very hard to appear pleasant and cheerful. She bantered with friends in the narthex. As she entered the sanctuary, she passed the notebook lying on the table where parishioners could submit prayer requests for the day. She thought fleetingly about asking for prayer, then changed her mind.

She took her place in the pew, and the service started. For the next hour, she struggled to shake off her fears. "I'm scared," she thought, "Tomorrow's MRI is bothering me a lot. Maybe I should have people pray for me."

After the sermon, the pastor customarily asked the congregation if anyone had prayer requests in addition to the ones listed in the bulletin and the prayer request notebook.

"I still don't know what came over me," Jane later reflected. "I raised my hand."

"This is an unusual request since most requests for prayer are prayers for others," Jane began. "But I am asking that you pray for me because I am having a brain scan this week. I think I am getting forgetful. I'm afraid of a tumor."

For a moment, a hush came over the congregation. The information was new to all who knew Jane. "It sounds scary," said the pastor. "We'll join in prayer for you." And so they did.

What happened as a result amazed Jane. After the divine service ended, many people came up to her to hug her or put their hand on her shoulder. One or two offered to come with her for the test. Many asked for the date and time so they could pray for her.

Jane took a risk in sharing her need with her congregation. The people of the congregation responded with concern and care. This is, of course, an example of an authentic encounter of one member with other members in a congregation. Jane wanted and needed support. She trusted, at least to some degree, the other members of her church. She identified her feelings of anxiety, and she talked about them. She shared what was happening to her. Together, these things formed the foundation for an authentic encounter.

Some organizations foster a culture in which authentic encounters happen spontaneously and often. In cultures like that, people more easily express and receive expressions of appreciation from one another. When relationships are genuine, statements of appreciation come across as genuine. Cultures like that are healthful for leaders and laity alike.

....

SCENE 4:

For several months, the Board of Elders at St. Martin's Church had been locked in a seemingly intractable series of conflicts. Members of the board felt more on edge for reasons that weren't quite clear, at least to Pastor Hal. The pastor knew all the members of the board quite well. He liked them, and felt frustrated that something was just not clicking. After a few weeks, he sat down to talk about this with his spiritual director, a wise pastor with many more years of ministry experience than Hal. Together, the two prayed about the situation and about Pastor Hal's leadership options.

When the board met the next evening, Pastor Hal decided to skip his usual opening devotion. Instead, he opened with this thought: "The apostle James teaches us that God hears and answers our prayers in powerful ways (James 5:16). Tonight I want to lead you in prayer for one another. As we go around the table, please share, if you would, something that's on your heart for which we can pray."

"It was like a spark had been kindled," Pastor Hal later thought. Elder after elder had spoken about personal worries and concerns: health, children and grandchildren, finances, friends.

Each took time to talk while the others listened. Each grew closer to the others as they shared. For an hour and forty-five minutes, the elders talked and prayed. Finally, they closed by singing the Common Doxology.

"No formal business was conducted," Pastor Hal thought as he walked to his car. "But our relationships grew."

In subsequent meetings, the board began in a similar way, sharing needs and praying together. After a time of prayer, the group made decisions on business items, handling them more efficiently than before. While differences remained, board conflicts became more productive as the group focused on finding creative solutions to problems.

"I really am moved by what you have helped us do Pastor Hal," said one elder several months later in a meeting. "I like the cohesion that praying together has created."

"Thanks," Pastor Hal responded, "The Spirit of God has moved us all to more openness and a deeper relationship with one another—all at the foot of Christ's cross. I am thankful to God and thankful to all of you for the personal risks you have taken to nourish and strengthen our relationships."

Openness and honesty are foundational for authentic encounter. Authenticity, in turn, makes it possible for people to receive the words and deeds of affirmation others offer us, interpreting them as meaningful. In one-on-one conversations, in small group interactions, in boards and meetings, in Bible study and prayer, members of the Christian community have opportunities to come to know one another more deeply, authentically, and genuinely. In so doing, they are also able to offer positive affirmation—affirmation that can take root.

Marriage counselors know that one significant predictor of success or failure in marriage is the ratio of positive to negative statements husbands and wives make to one another in their day-to-day conversations. The more negativity in a relationship, the more likely that relationship will remain distant and, eventually, dissolve. The more positivity in a relationship, the more likely the relationship will endure and deepen. The increased bonding that results from positive statements helps people to manage the inevitable challenges that arise in any relationship.

When churches become communities in which authentic relationships form, when believers meet at the foot of the cross and in the power of Christ's empty tomb, when people seek one another out to affirm one another, powerful bonds form. Many more positive statements than negative ones are spoken. In short, members look for things others are doing well and affirm them. The culture grows more healthy for everyone, especially church workers.

SPEAKING PERSONALLY

Growing up in an alcoholic family, I learned the keep-your-feelings-to-yourself rule very well. My mom warned me never to talk about my dad's drinking. After all, "What would people think?" I learned that other people likely would not understand what we were going through, and therefore they could not be trusted. I learned that I should be grateful I had a roof over my head and food to eat. I learned not to want things to get better. After all, this was our family's lot in life. Authentic encounters were not really possible. There was always a great reality hidden.

It has taken a lot of work to identify what I feel and actually think. It has taken even more work to share with others some of my experiences. In the process, I have begun to understand that all human beings have a deep need for authentic connection.

Isn't this authentic connection the very nature of the Christian community? We grow as people in the context of relationship with others. As others engage with me at the deeper levels of my being, I am touched, moved, and, by God's grace, grow.

Over the years, I have also discovered that facing failure is scary. Throughout life, I have tended to avoid hearing about the problems I am causing others. But as people have engaged me in deeper relationships, they have affirmed my basic worth as a child of God. They have affirmed the gifts God has given me. This affirmation makes it easier for me to listen when they confront me with actions that are problematic in some way.

In the earlier days of my marriage I think I was more prone to give voice to disappointments and criticisms than I was to give voice to positive support and appreciation. This put an unnecessary strain on our marriage, as the research suggests. Over time I've looked for more positives. I have learned to like looking for the positives. In a very small way, it must be a little like it is with God, who sees us through the atoning lens of His Son, Jesus.

CHAPTER SEVEN

EMPHASIZING HEALTH AND WELL-BEING

SCENE 1:

Pastor John sat in his office at St. Matthew's working on his sermon. The phone rang. When Pastor answered, a distraught, elderly parishioner told him hurriedly that the ambulance was on its way to her home. Her husband was being taken to the emergency room, suffering from what looked like a broken hip. Pastor John prayed briefly with her, grabbed his Bible and prayer book, and drove to the hospital. For several hours, he cared for the family, praying for healing, courage, and faith in Christ's presence. "This is what pastors do," he said to himself as he left the hospital to return to his office, "and I am honored to be able to serve God in this way."

SCENE 2:

Pastor John sat in his office at St. Matthew's working on his sermon. He looked up to see three members of his congregation slowly jogging past his window. By now, they had made several laps around the parking lot and would soon move on to a nearby park. He knew all three of them well, and he knew they had made a pact to build better cardiovascular endurance by exercising more. They had gotten the idea to support one another in this way because of a recent congregational emphasis: "Body, Mind, And Spirit—Looking at Our Life And Community in Holistic Ways."

Pastor John got up, grabbed his Bible and prayer book, and made his way across the parking lot to intercept them. As they saw him approach, they slowed, but he encouraged them to keep running in place. He prayed briefly with them for healing, courage, and faith in Christ's presence.

As he made his way back to the office, he told himself, "This is what pastors do, and I am honored to be able to serve God in this way."

....

SCENE 3:

Sarah, the administrative assistant at St. Matthew's, had heard Pastor John take the call from the elderly parishioner and then leave for the hospital. Later that afternoon, she looked out her window and saw him praying with the jogging threesome. A bit surprised, it brought a concern to her mind. It wasn't the first time.

"Pastor is such a blessing," she thought, "He's such a good pastor. He's been wonderful for this congregation. But . . ." When Pastor John returned from the parking lot, Sarah followed him into his office.

"Pastor," Sarah began, "I saw you talking with the three joggers. And I was thinking . . . I'm concerned about the pace you keep, and, honestly, about the weight you carry. Have you thought at all about joining them? Or doing something else more active like that? You're such a great pastor, and I'm a little worried about your health. What do you think?"

At first, Pastor John felt a bit stunned. He frowned and took a deep breath. Then, sensing Sarah's concern and remembering his congregation's emphasis on health and well-being for all its members, he recovered a bit. "Thanks for your concern, Sarah," he responded.

"Well, okay, Pastor," Sarah replied. "But can we talk about a next step?"

"Maybe I'll get together with our parish nurse and my doctor to talk about this. Maybe I can get an exercise program started," Pastor John mused.

And so he did. Sarah was overjoyed—and so were Pastor John's wife, his adolescent children, and several other members of the parish.

A month later there were four joggers, one a bit slower than the rest. While they jogged, they sometimes sang hymns and prayed.

Pastor John, Sarah, the three joggers, the ill husband, and the concerned spouse were all members of the Christian community at St. Matthew's. The scenarios above all illustrate key characteristics of that kind of community.

First, the community (represented in this case by Pastor John), responded quickly and directly to the medical emergency faced by two of its members. Attentive to the healing ministry of Jesus Himself and remembering the words of the apostle in James 5, congregations instinctively expect to have this kind of an outreach to their members. In this case, it's likely that members of a visitation team will follow up with the elderly couple.

Second, Pastor John responded quickly and directly to the new health-enhancing behaviors of three members. Doing so is perhaps less instinctive in many congregations, but they need not be. St. Matthew's had just finished a congregation-wide study focused on the truth that God empowers us to steward our health throughout life so that we can live out the full potential of joy and service He intends.

Through this study, too, members had begun more intentionally and holistically to address health issues among their membership. Several boards had discussed how the congregation might hold a health fair for both its members and members of the surrounding community. They had begun to explore other ways to invest in the health and well-being concerns of the community in which the congregation is located. Some members hope that health-focused activities and resources will provide an innovative way to carry out evangelism outreach.

In this context, the three joggers made their pact. Before they had gained a theological understanding of the stewardship of and care for their bodies, physical health hadn't been much of a concern. Now, they had made it a priority to focus on their physical well-being, and to do so with friends in a group of three that, as we have seen, soon became four.

Spurred on by this congregation-wide emphasis, several of St. Matthew's members in health care vocations (two nurses, a nutritionist, an exercise coach, and a social worker/counselor) came forward to create a Congregational Health and Well-being Committee. Some people in this group have questioned the practice of serving gooey donuts between services. Was this sending the right health message? In addition, the nurses had offered to provide occasional screening services like those often offered in a more formal parish nurse program.

These are great outcomes! However, at this point, no one had made explicit provision for encouraging health-enhancing behaviors on the part of the church staff at St. Matthew's. This brings to mind a third helpful aspect of St. Matthew's approach, described in the conversation between Sarah and Pastor John: already enjoying a close working relationship between herself and her pastor, and encouraged by the congregational study on health and well-being, Sarah felt safe in encouraging Pastor John to join the joggers.

In authentic communities, members share an interest in and a genuine concern for one another. Sarah addressed her concern for Pastor John's health and well-being directly with him. Her words resulted in the pastor taking an important step toward improved health. Sarah was not judgmental. She spoke out of true concern, not as a member of the congregation's "health police." Her inquiry did not come out of the blue. Instead, it was embedded in a larger picture, the congregation's recent study. Thus, Pastor John did not feel singled out. The conversation flowed naturally from the context.

This leads into the fourth and final point drawn from the vignettes that began this chapter: for maximum effectiveness, care for church workers must embed itself in a broader, congregation-wide emphasis. Pastors, teachers, and other workers need not (and should not!) be singled out. Thus, such an emphasis does not emerge from an initiative such as "St. Matthew's Church cares for the health and well-being of its workers." Rather, care for church workers emerges from a more general congregational value, a value expressed in language such as this: "St. Matthew's Church cares for the health and well-being of its members and of all those people in the community it serves. Among the people it cares for in focused and intentional ways are its workers."

Well people are aware of their need to develop the whole self. This requires attention to one's spiritual, physical, emotional, intellectual, social/interpersonal, and vocational well-being. Congregational health and well-being committees encourage and enable their members to maintain a high quality of life in each of these dynamics. Dr. Thomas Droege notes:

Health leaders recognize that future improvements in health will come about only as people assume greater responsibility for their health and for the health of their communities. This is a spiritual problem calling for changes in behavior, not a medical problem calling for a scientific breakthrough. National health leaders are challenging churches to rediscover their commitment to health and healing, a commitment that is deeply embedded in the tradition of Christianity. When faithful to their mission, churches address the personal and social moral issues that people face, including issues of health and social justice. As Christians committed to the promotion of better health for persons and communities, we share a common mission and core values with health leaders . . . [1]

The overall attitude of care for the health and well-being of each individual in the congregation and community is central to the support of church workers. The congregation's focus is clear: we are in the business of eternal salvation and in living here-and-now in the fullness Christ's salvation brings as we await the end time. Martin Luther may have had this kind of stewardship of life emphasis in mind when he wrote:

I believe that God has made me and all creatures; that He has given me my body and soul, eyes, ears, and all my members, my reason and all my senses, and still takes care of them. . . . For all this it is my duty to thank and praise, serve and obey Him. (Small Catechism, First Article of the Apostles' Creed)

SPEAKING PERSONALLY

My vocation has focused on remediation. My personality, the models of pastoral care I have studied, and the counseling techniques I have learned all lead me to identify problems and then work to address them. Thus, I tend to focus more on what's already wrong than on prevention.

My own focus on pathology (the problem side of things) is mirrored by the health care system in the United States. We spend 95 percent of our medical dollars on healing disease and only 5 percent on prevention and wellness. I'm so problem-focused that it took a personal challenge from someone I deeply respect to get me to confront my own thinking.

Dr. Lois Klatt, emeritus professor of exercise physiology and kinesiology at Concordia University Chicago, has been a mentor for me for many years. At one point, she asked me, "Bruce, why is it that churches pray in public for people who are sick, but we never ask God to support, protect, and encourage people who are doing things to help themselves stay well?"

I really had no answer. Lois continued: "Why do we not pray for people who are beginning and continuing exercise programs? Or for those who intend to move away from fast foods and toward healthier fruits and vegetables?"

"Why," she asked, "do we wait for problems to develop before we'll pray? Shouldn't we ask God to help people prevent problems and pray for them during their work at prevention?"

Nothing like this had ever occurred to me before, but

Lois had made a powerful point and, frankly, I was convinced.

Many conversations with Lois helped enlarge my vision of what was possible in congregations. Gathered around Word and Sacrament beneath the cross of our Savior, we meet together as people who are sinful, wounded, and ill. The Gospel speaks to that, of course. But it also speaks to us as people who, under God's blessing, can grow and mature as children of God. I am one of those people— sinful, wounded, and ill, while at the same time, capable of growth and of maturing as a child of God.

Early in my pastoral counseling career, I attended

> **WHEN PEOPLE IN THE BODY OF CHRIST ENGAGE AND SUPPORT ONE ANOTHER IN AUTHENTIC CONCERN AND COMPASSION, HEALTHY BEHAVIORS ARE MORE LIKELY TO RESULT.**

several small group retreats. Each time as I returned, I thought about what had happened at the retreat and tried to implement productive change, based on what I had learned. It was a frustrating experience. I was only one person, a voice crying out in the wilderness, so to speak. Though others tried to understand what I was so enthusiastically advocating, I couldn't make it clear. Though they wanted to support the changes I wanted to make, they didn't know how.

Since then, I have learned that research supports my personal experience. Many studies show that if change is to occur, there must be ongoing support for that change "back home." Similarly, if we expect church workers to implement health-enhancing changes, those changes must be supported and encouraged in the specific contexts in which those workers daily find themselves. When the people in my community, the people who are close to me, support the changes I want to make, those changes are more likely to happen.

This all reminds me of how I stopped smoking. For decades—since high school, in fact—I had smoked a pipe. Like most smokers, I had made several private resolutions to stop, all of which failed. Then one day my two sons confronted me. They had just finished a health class in school, and they asked me if I knew what I was doing to my body. Having my sons talk with me so directly and with such concern made a powerful impact.

Here's the point: when people in the Body of Christ engage and support one another in authentic concern and compassion, healthy behaviors are more likely to result.

CHAPTER EIGHT

WORKER SUPPORT TEAMS

SCENE 1:

The leadership of St. Mark's was struggling. Contributions were lagging among its membership of 400 or so; attendance at worship was holding its own at about 175 a week, but doing so with newer and younger families that did not have the financial resources of their elders. Challenging the budget further still was the fact that many older members had cut back on their giving as they grew more and more reliant on fixed incomes.

There was, to say the least, anxiety in the air as Ben, chairperson of the finance committee, called their second meeting to order.

The first meeting had been tense. As everyone poured over next year's budget, comparing expenses with St. Mark's projected income, one thing seemed clear: in the coming year, bills would exceed income. The committee faced a daunting task.

"A large portion of our budget is for personnel," Ben remembered one member saying. Ben didn't want to venture down that path, but off they went. "If we reduced the pastor's salary just a little, say 5 percent, and also moved to a less expensive option in our health plan, we could save enough to balance the budget."

Ben looked at Pastor Luke, who had opened the meeting with a brief devotion and prayer. The pastor had not said a word at that first meeting, until he closed it with prayer. "I wonder what he was thinking," Ben thought to himself.

What was Pastor Luke thinking? "I am in a very difficult spot," Luke thought to himself. "I'd like to speak against this salary reduction, but if I do, it will look self-serving. I want to be a servant leader, so I'll just keep quiet. But, frankly, I'm stretching to keep my head above the financial water now. A 5 percent cut would press my budget even harder. God will never give us more than we can bear. I know that, or at least I preach it, but this could really be a problem. And it's irritating too."

Later that evening when Pastor Luke shared the finance committee's conversation with his wife, Lydia, there was something of an eruption. "I basically manage the money," Lydia said with considerable force, "and I'm not sure we can absorb something like that! What are they thinking? Doesn't anyone understand how difficult this will be for our family?"

Pastor Luke retreated to his study, but he couldn't stop the thoughts cascading through his mind. "I wonder who will stand up for me? Will anyone?

Maybe I should just open the meeting and then excuse myself. That might make it easier for them to talk about my compensation."

....

SCENE 1 (AN ALTERNATIVE VERSION):

The leadership of St. Mark's was struggling. Contributions were lagging among its membership of 400 or so; attendance at worship was holding its own at about 175 a week, but doing so with newer and younger families that did not have the financial resources of their elders. Challenging the budget further still was the fact that many older members had cut back on their giving as they grew more and more reliant on fixed incomes.

There was, to say the least, anxiety in the air as Ben, chairperson of the finance committee, called their second meeting to order.

The first meeting had been tense. As everyone poured over next year's budget, comparing expenses with St. Mark's projected income, one thing seemed clear: expenses would likely exceed income. The committee faced a daunting task.

"A large portion of our budget is for personnel," Ben remembered one member saying. "Hold on," Ben had replied. "We have agreed that whenever we take up issues of salaries and benefits, we will invite a member or two of our Worker Support

Team (WST). They are the appointed advocates for the workers who serve at St. Mark's."

Heads nodded around the table. The WST had been formed about a year ago. The church had chartered it to advocate for the health and well-being of those who serve at St. Mark's. The finance committee had agreed that every discussion of "worker issues" would include at least one member of this committee.

Ben looked at Pastor Luke, who had opened the meeting with a brief devotion and prayer. Pastor had not said a word until he had closed the meeting with prayer. "I wonder what he was thinking," Ben thought to himself.

What was Pastor Luke thinking? "I'm really glad the WST was formed," the pastor thought. "Over the past year, the WST has talked with me in increasingly genuine ways about how I'm doing and how my being in the ministry at St. Mark's is working out for Lydia and for our children too. The WST members have a deep sense of this, and can articulate it. It will be a huge blessing if one or two of them can come to the next finance committee meeting."

Now, Ben was calling the second finance committee meeting to order. After the opening devotion and prayer, Ben announced, "Since we will be discussing staff salary and benefits, we're happy to welcome two members of the Worker Support Team. I'd also like to give Pastor Luke the opportunity to leave. I suspect it might be uncomfortable for you to listen as we hash all this through, Pastor. You're welcome to stay, of course. But you are also welcome to leave."

Pastor Luke stood. "I'm thankful for the presence of the WST members," he said. "I'm sure they can speak on behalf of my family and me." Then he left, entrusting his concerns to the WST representatives.

These two scenarios differ in fundamental ways. In the first, the pastor stood alone. With no one to speak up for him, he could either advocate for himself (leaving himself open to charges of being self-centered and self-serving) or he could simply keep quiet and let events take their course.

In the second scenario, the pastor could trust the advocacy of people specifically appointed for that task. Because of their work together over the past year, these people were ready and willing to represent his needs in the emerging conversation about salary and benefits.

More than twenty years ago, the Wisconsin Evangelical Lutheran Synod began to study ways to enhance the quality of life of church workers and workers' families. They recommended that each congregation create a Care Committee for Church Workers. They also developed a handbook to assist churches in doing so. Today, CCCW committees exist at the national, district, and congregational levels. Their stated purpose is "to monitor and address each called worker's spiritual, emotional, professional, and physical needs."[1] The CCCW committees

■ evaluate the salaries and benefits received by called workers;

■ host staff fellowship activities;

■ provide guidance on behalf of called workers as the personnel handbook is developed or revised;

■ respond to physical or emotional illness or incapacity;

■ evaluate position descriptions to determine if the congregation's and workers' needs are being attended to.

Similarly, in 1988, the Evangelical Lutheran Church in America developed a model congregational constitution that prominently included a Staff Support Committee. Such a group in each congregation would

■ open communication about expectations, attitudes, and concerns within the congregation, the community, and the staff;

■ identify early warning signs of misunderstandings;

■ become a "listening post" for the pastor, the associate in ministry, and the people;

■ serve as a group with whom the pastor and associate in ministry could test new ideas and share confidential matters;

■ conduct annual views and affirmations of staff;

■ be a sounding board for the pastor and associate in ministry in times of personal or professional stress and in times of congregational crisis;

■ plan continuing education and sabbaticals that benefited both the mission of the congregation and the ministry of the staff;

■ assess each year the working conditions, compensation, housing, and benefits provided to the pastor and associate in ministry.[2]

In the experience of the ELCA with this model, it is

reported that continuing to pair evaluation issues with support issues has caused some difficulties. A newer resource was issued in 2003, *Pastor and People: Making Mutual Ministry Work*. This small edited volume is full of practical suggestions that help in the task of "tending the relationship between pastor and people" (p. 15).

In the United Methodist Church, evaluation and support continue to be kept together in a small book by Gwen Purushotham, *Watching Over One Another in Love: A Wesleyan Model for Ministry Assessment*. Purushotham maintains that both nurture and accountability are indivisible aspects of the overall support process and are both gifts given by God to enhance congregational life in the Body of Christ.

Thus, the call for a focused group of people in the congregation whose function is to hold up the arms of the prophets and support church workers is not idiosyncratic or unique.

WHO IN YOUR CONGREGATION ADVOCATES FOR CHURCH WORKERS?

Who in your congregation advocates for church workers? Who addresses their concerns? Within the Body of Christ, members care for one another. Yet if everyone in general cares for everyone in general, church workers can easily fall off the radar screen. When everyone is responsible, no one is responsible.

How To Start Your Own Committee

- Whatever you call this care team, committee, or task force, it should include individuals who have a heart for staff and for the families of staff members who are married. Such a committee should create a safe environment for mutual planning and prayer. Such a group will work to enhance the effectiveness of church workers, supporting their health and well-being and advocating for them when it would be inappropriate or awkward for them to advocate for themselves.

- Members of the committee should have a heart for worker care and support. As such committees are constituted, the congregation's leaders may want to consider the inclusion of church members with special skills when available. For example, members trained in the behavioral sciences (e.g., social workers, counselors, psychologists) could enhance the committee's effectiveness, as could human resource professionals, health and wellness educators, and physical fitness trainers. Financial planners and time management coaches could make fine members too. But most important, they need a heart for worker care and support.

- Consider including people of different ages and both genders on such a team. Voices from different perspectives will prove most helpful in the ongoing conversation, utilizing the diverse gifts found in the Body of Christ.

■ Additionally, the committee should connect in an intentional way to the governance of the congregation. This means that at least one member (but preferably two or three) of this committee should serve on another pertinent board or committee (e.g., Elders, School Board, Governance Council, Finance Committee).

Note, though, that not all care committee members should serve on congregational governance groups. Voices independent of the governance structure are very important.

The care committee in each congregation will develop its own style and pacing, but at a minimum, it should meet with every worker individually once every six months for at least 90 minutes. This sets a tone and makes a statement about the importance of the worker's well-being.

In the beginning, though, the committee should meet one-on-one with workers more often, perhaps every three months. The goal should be getting to know the worker and developing authentic trust. One or more of these meetings could well include the worker's spouse and children. Of course, if concerns emerge, the care committee will meet more often.

What happens when the care committee meets with a worker? Conversation should revolve around three basic questions: (1) How are you doing, and how is the work going? (2) What areas are going especially well in your life, both professionally and personally? (3) What areas both professionally and personally need attention? (Section 3 will address care committee agendas in much more detail.)

Note that care committees like those described above aren't formed with the intent of solving a particular problem with a worker, especially as that "problem" is perceived by the congregation's leadership. It would be a mistake to initiate a care committee in the midst of a crisis. Rather, a care committee emerges out of an overall strategy of care; care for congregation members, as well as for church workers. Such a committee also emerges because congregations recognize the particular vulnerabilities and dangers faced by its faithful and effective workers. When care committee members have a heart for church workers and when they focus their efforts on worker health, those efforts will prove life-enhancing for both the worker and the congregation.

The existence of such a committee tells everyone that the congregation values its workers, their health, and their well-being. Without such a committee, church workers are left to fend for themselves. They must rely on spontaneous expressions of care rather than on a clear statement by the congregation that their well-being is a significant priority. In this sense, the existence of such a committee is, in itself, an expression of support.

To sum up, the central charge of the Worker Support Team is to encourage, foster, advocate, and plan for the health and well-being of church staff in authentic partnership and conversation with them.

SPEAKING PERSONALLY

Over the years, I have come alongside many church workers who saw themselves as all alone in their ministry, workers who had few advocates and little support in the congregations or schools they served. I have tried to walk with them through their pain and, often, their depression and despair. As I listened and counseled, I thought a lot about where they might look for advocacy and support.

Whether their sense of being alone in their struggles was real or imagined, whether advocacy and support were actually available or not, their struggles were real. And those struggles sapped the energy both of the worker and that person's congregation as well.

I've sometimes even wondered if perhaps church workers should unionize! Though I never took that idea too seriously, I cannot escape the urgency I feel as I think about the need for worker advocates in every congregation.

From these musings emerged the idea of the advocacy and care groups I have described in this chapter. As I researched the possibilities, I was delighted to discover that some church bodies had already begun the kind of work I envisioned. I've noted the results of some of that research above. It really is high time for every congregation to attend to the needs of church workers and to put in place structures to support such attention.

In the mid-1990s, the parochial school teachers in the Archdiocese of St. Louis battled with the Archdiocese around salary issues. In desperation, the teachers finally took out a full-page ad in the *St. Louis Post-Dispatch* comparing teacher pay in the Archdiocese with teacher pay in the St. Louis public schools. The contrast was stunning, and the ad accomplished what the teachers intended; it ended the impasse.

I am not suggesting that church workers take out full-page ads all over the country. But I do believe that the voices of our workers need to be heard. Often that requires someone to advocate on their behalf.

I know that in my own life I need people who are genuinely interested in my well-being, who seek to understand me, and who, in some cases at least, are willing to go to bat for me. I realize that even when they go to bat, they might not get a hit, and I might not gain all I wish, but at least I have a voice. My concerns have been understood, and, with Christ at my side and members of His Body as fellow travelers, I can walk in hope and confidence.

CHAPTER NINE

PROMISES, COVENANTS, AND ACCOUNTABILITY

SCENE 1:

George felt perturbed. Things just weren't the same since Pastor Will and the church's preschool director, Brenda, had retired. Both had worked together for over a decade, and under their stable leadership, everything had flowed along smoothly.

George liked knowing what to expect on a Sunday morning, though, truth be told, Pastor Will's sermons had seemed to lack some steam in the last couple of years. The school held its own, even when several challenging students from the neighborhood had enrolled. Brenda's consistent and even discipline helped a lot in that regard, George supposed.

Slowly George had warmed up a bit to the new pastor, Pastor Ed. Still, it was hard to adjust to such a difference in styles. From the pulpit, Pastor Ed talked about things like human feelings, struggles, and the like. "Pastors shouldn't be talking about such dark things during the sermon," Sam opined to his friend Brett. "I really don't like his style."

George also had his doubts about the new pre-school director, Liz. "Did you know she wants to open the school up?" George asked Brett. "She thinks we should work harder to recruit students who are a lot different than our current members. What if those parents want to join the congregation? I know I shouldn't feel this way, but it's so unfamiliar. I'm starting to feel like this isn't my church anymore."

Brett took a deep breath. "Well, George," he began, "it sounds like you've got a lot of reactions—both feelings and thoughts—to our new staff. It sounds as if you don't like the changes you see and the changes that might be coming."

"Exactly!" responded George.

Brett cleared his throat and continued. "When we had those small group meetings last year, we agreed on how we would handle differences like this. Right?"

George saw where Brett was going. He squirmed a bit as Brett continued: "We agreed together as a congregation that whenever we had a disagreement, we would first talk with the person involved. If that didn't clear it up, there were other steps to take. I don't think you've taken the first step yet. I think you need to take up your concerns with Pastor Ed and Director Liz."

"I'm not ready to do that," muttered George.

"It's what we agreed to do," replied Brett.

"Pastor won't listen," George said hastily, retreating a bit.

"Maybe he will and maybe he won't, but we agreed on what we would do," Brett said, not giving an inch.

"Well, I just can't do that yet," said George, a bit defiant.

"Think about it, George, and I'll pray about it too," Brett responded.

"Sure," said George, glad to end the conversation.

But before they parted, Brett added, "You know, George, we also agreed that if someone talked to us about someone else, we would bring that to the attention of the third party. So you should know that I intend to tell Pastor Ed and Director Liz about this conversation. I'm going to encourage them to phone you."

"All right!" replied George, "You don't have to do that. I'll talk with them."

"Great," replied Brett. "Please let me know when you've made the contact, so that I know I have done my part."

"Will do," said George. "By the way, as you can tell, this has not been the most comfortable conversation I've had in my life. But I think it's important. And I want to thank you for calling me to account over it. We did agree to do this. I appreciate your helping me remember that."

"You're welcome," responded a relieved Brett. "I will keep praying about it. And if I can help at all in the conversation, please let me know. I appreciate your openness."

Both men smiled, shook hands, and went their separate ways. George was true to his word. He called both Pastor Ed and Director Liz, made appointments with each of them, and also reported back to Brett.

Brett and George both belong to a congregation that has worked to put in place a behavioral covenant. In groups large and small, congregation leaders talked with one another over the better part of a year, then they crafted the statement of agreement Brett described in the conversation above. In working through this process, they have answered the questions, "How will we act when we don't understand one another? What will we do when we don't agree with one another?" The statement they developed describes an approach to conflict resolution that is aligned with biblical teaching and supportive of courteous conversation and civil behaviors. [1]

In contrast to laws, covenants are agreements or promises. Staffs, congregational leaders, and even whole congregations can agree on how they will behave with one another. The accent lies on behaviors, not on personalities or values. This emphasis is crucial, because even in the Christian community so many behaviors can be excused if they are framed in pious-sounding words. The question is, "How will we act toward one another?" And then, "How will we hold one another accountable for the behaviors we have agreed to adopt?"

For example, one church in Illinois has adopted four principles for sharing hurts and disagreements in congregational life:

1. Tell the truth

2. Avoid gossip

3. Remain faithful

4. Address conflict.[2]

This congregation has agreed on how they will live together. They have committed to truth-telling, direct conversation (avoiding gossip), faithful living, and a direct approach to conflict. Following this model, people like George and Brett in the example above have a way to challenge gossip in relatively safe ways. Those who violate the principles that govern life in their faith community can be held accountable. When the emphasis lies on behavior, it does not matter if the cause is just. The ends do not justify the means when a covenant like this is being violated.

Martin Luther reminds us of our need to attend to the underlying motivations of negative or evil behavior in pious surroundings:

> The white, good-looking devil is the one who does
> the most harm, the devil who eggs people on to

> commit spiritual sins, which are not regarded as
> sins at all but as pure righteousness and are de-
> fended as such. He causes more harm that the
> dark devil, who only eggs people on to commit
> gross, carnal sins, which are so obviously sins that
> even Turks and heathen can recognize them as
> such.[3]

The real task is to attend to what people do, as well as to what people say. Behavioral covenants or agreements attend to the doing. Thus, they are focused on enhancing relationships between members in the Body of Christ.

Does the culture affect the church? Absolutely! Unfortunately, though, we often think of culture's influences as being primarily a cognitive assault. To be sure, the world around us does promote doctrinal errors and false beliefs. It does attack the person and work of our Savior, the authority of the Scripture, and a myriad of moral absolutes. These kinds of assault draw most of our attention. We notice and discuss the world's influence on our behaviors far less often. But that influence can cause equal harm!

Increasingly, our society endorses an "in your face" style. It applauds impulsive and reactive ways of speaking and relating. One person yells at another "because he was wrong and ignorant." One person physically abuses another "because she was not submitting to me as head of the household." Talk show guests shout one another down. Attack ads determine the outcome of elections. Negative blogs trash reputations.

When this relational style creeps into the church, our churches become mirrors of the culture. They offer no spiritually vital, vibrant alternative. In addition, members and church workers alike have no safe space in which to give and receive care. Everyone must be on guard at all times.

Behavioral covenants or agreements bring some sense of promise, order, expectation, and accountability into relationships. They also draw members of the community into direct discussion about their behavior and its effects on others.

In addition to behavioral covenants, most denominations and a few congregations have established a formal grievance procedure. Under such an arrangement, when one member of the congregation has a concern or problem with another member or with a staff member, it triggers the process. Having a basic framework for addressing grievances gives individuals a way to find redress for hurts and injustices, real or imagined. This can keep frustration over minor issues from escalating into serious conflicts.

Grievance procedures should be clear and, ideally, simple. They should be based on Scripture and align with existing polity and bylaws. Everyone in the congregation should know about them.

Behavioral covenants or agreements, holy manners, and explicit grievance procedures all contribute to the well-being of church workers. Where such agreements are in place, people know what to expect from one another and how to go about processing differences.

Here's an example of a behavioral covenant from which a Worker Support Team could began its work. It aligns with the purposes Chapter 8 outlines for WSTs, to "encourage, foster, advocate, and plan for the health and well-being of the workers of our church in authentic partnership and conversation with them."

We promise to . . .

- hold every member of our Worker Support Team and every worker of our church in prayer regularly;

- rejoice in the presence of Christ in our conversations, and pray that Christ's Spirit will wash over all we do;

- attend faithfully to the task given to us and remain focused on it, avoiding involvement in responsibilities assigned to other groups in our church;

- begin our work together in sharing and prayer, being as forthright as possible about our own lives so that we can effectively support one another;

- end our work together in debriefing and prayer, sharing our responses to what we have done together, including any effect on our personal relationships;

- respect one another's schedules by beginning and ending on time;

- listen carefully and as fully as possible to others so as to understand their positions, ideas, and concerns, prioritizing listening over speaking;

- fully involve the church workers in our conversations so that we are always talking with rather than about them;

- stay alert to joys and concerns members of the congregation share about our workers and, when hearing such, to offer the WST table as a place for discussion according to our congregational covenants;

- take time out if any conversation becomes too heated, using the time for reflection and prayer;
- encourage and allow the space and freedom for everyone to have voice at our meetings;
- share our thoughts and our feelings in the meeting, avoiding personal silence during the meeting and gossip thereafter;
- practice confession and absolution as part of our ongoing work together, asking for forgiveness when appropriate and witnessing to Christ's forgiveness and our own as well;
- speak publicly in support of the decisions of the WST even if those decisions were not ones we personally promoted;
- work toward consensus in our work rather than resorting to votes;
- assess and evaluate our work together on a regular basis, taking time to do so in a deeper way than is possible in each meeting's regular debriefing time.

This agreement is not perfect, nor is it all-inclusive. Still, the group finds it helpful to review it briefly each time they meet. Every few months, the group uses it to evaluate their work. One way they have done this is to list each promise on paper, along with a rating scale each member fills out independently. Then the group tallies the ratings and talks about them. For instance,

To begin and end on time

This is a challenge				This is going well
1	2	3	4	5

This kind of a process builds in an automatic opportunity for reflection about the WST's work and members' relationships with one another. Building it in underscores its value and importance.

SPEAKING PERSONALLY

It's hard to express the personal pain I have felt when destructive behaviors were ignored in meetings. It is equally difficult to find words for my sadness as I've watched members of the Body of Christ behave in destructive ways toward one another, all the while using pious terms and theological language to justify themselves. Arguing for the "correct" position gives no one the right to steamroll over the feelings and sensitivities of others.

Distressing though those things have been, it is even harder to carry the burden of knowing that at times I, too, have played a part in the bad behaviors, either by actively participating or by my silence, passively allowing such behaviors to continue. As I walk with others, humbled by Christ's cross and empowered by His resurrection, mutual accountability has become for me more and more a key component of life in the community called together by Christ.

As a seminary instructor, I ask my students to come to

me if things I do in class, the way that I teach, my personal style, or my words trouble them. Effective learning calls for my students and me to live together as allies in our mutual task. To be true to this covenant, however, I need to seriously consider the feedback my students offer. I must be willing to change in ways large or small.

My goal is not to have a process that looks good from the outside. Instead, I want to foster authentic relationships where more the internal reality dictates the external look. I want to engage the power of the Holy Spirit so that all of us are open to acknowledging our sin, pleading for Christ's forgiveness, and asking for forgiveness from others in the class. Only then can we give and receive the wonderful assurance of Christ's ongoing love for us and our mutual care and love for one another.

Working to put behavioral covenants, promises, or agreements in place and then acting on them has been difficult for me. My upbringing militates against it, as does the individualistic culture rampant in both the church and society. I am often tempted to think I have a right to do what I want when I want to do it, to say whatever is on my mind, regardless of its effect on others.

My own resistance reminds me of why I wrote this chapter. It calls me and, I hope, it calls other believers to a higher vision of the Christian community. It calls us beyond a simple task-orientation in which doing trumps care. It calls us to walk away from the temptation to get our own way by using manipulation and power. It urges us toward the kind of self-giving love Jesus has in mind for the members of His Body.

I pray that the Holy Spirit will continue to work in all of us, leading us to find the better way, the way of Christ who entered our human experience to redeem it and us.

What Can Congregations Do?

The best thing congregations, schools, and other institutions can do for their workers is to live together in healthy ways. When that happens, helpful policies, encouraging ideas, and random acts of support flow naturally. Such a culture enhances the well-being of every worker—and of every volunteer too!

Christ gathers His people together around Word and Sacrament. There, His Holy Spirit is at work. Congregations are not random gatherings, connected by mere circumstance. They are people in a community created by Christ, people to whom God has given diverse gifts, people who, though fallen, nevertheless should be able to expect sanctified behaviors as they interact with one another.

As congregations, schools, and other Christian institutions grow healthier, they will experience more genuine relationships between and among individual members, relationships that demonstrate Christlike love. They will care about the general health and well-being of each member. They will attend not only to what they say but also to the ways they behave. They will hold one another accountable and they will welcome that accountability.

As that happens, they will look for tools to help them in the quest to care more effectively for one another, especially their workers. This section of the book will explain several of these tools and how to use them.

The first tool is the Wholeness Wheel (see p 129). It encourages each Christian to live in light of our Baptism, realizing that God has placed us into a new relationship with Himself and with one another. This fact has implications for every facet of our lives. Helping church workers think through each of these facets is a helpful tactic, one that should be a major focus as the Worker Support Team (WST) in each congregation does its work.

Second, we will return to the burnout discussion of Chapter Three and explore its implications in more depth. It will help us think about ways to develop church worker support systems.

Third, we will focus on the biblical concept of spiritual armor. Building on what some have called "faith hardiness," we will consider how such hardiness develops and in what environments. WST members will find many practical ideas in this chapter.

Fourth, we will study the question of compensation and consider how it leads to or detracts from worker well-being. It will help congregations develop strategies for dealing with salaries and benefits.

Fifth, we will think about how church workers manage their time and the expectations of the congregation for how they should do this. These are twin issues, and it is helpful to consider them together.

Last, we will present ideas WSTs will find helpful as

they seek to support church workers by caring for the worker's spouse and family.

Each tool in this section of the book will help congregations craft a supportive context that will contribute to the well-being of church workers. Throughout, the text will refer to the role of the congregation's Worker Support Team. When a group like this carries specific responsibility for understanding, developing, and using the tools described, worker well-being is likely to stay on the front burner. When everyone in the church or on the Church Council carries the responsibility, chances are that no one will take specific, helpful action. To put it another way, if support of church workers is seen as a vital and necessary task, then specific people will need to step forward, take specific actions, and hold themselves specifically accountable for follow-through.

Random acts of caring are important and very much appreciated by most church workers. Retreats and time away certainly help too. But they can't help as much as having a regular safe space in which to share needs and frustrations. It is good stewardship to care for the people whom God has created, Christ has redeemed, and the Spirit has called into service.

....

CHAPTER TEN

THE WHOLENESS WHEEL

What is the opposite of *wholeness*? Partedness? Dividedness? Or perhaps unintegratedness?

Compartmentalization captures the condition well, perhaps even most effectively of all. Both wholeness and compartmentalization are actually ways of looking at one's existence, ways of categorizing and organizing life and behaviors.

When we compartmentalize, we allow different segments of life to stand apart from one another, never touching or integrating to form a whole. For instance, if someone believes that personal faith belongs only in the heart and in the church building, one's faith is compartmentalized. It belongs here (in the church) but not there (in the workplace or the home).

If a church worker exhausts himself in the service of the church and then has no energy to engage the vocation of husband or father, that worker has compartmentalized his life. To defend this by saying, "I must serve God first," compartmentalizes "service to God" as something that happens only at church, not at home.

If a church worker leads effectively, bringing energy, charisma, and excitement to her school, but has no personal devotional life, claiming that effective leadership takes all her time and energy, then the worker is compartmentalizing vocational effectiveness and her own spiritual life and well-being.

If a church worker insists on using tobacco, reasoning, "it relaxes me," and refusing to recognize the damage tobacco use does to one's physical well-being, then that person is separating the physical and emotional parts of life, ignoring the fact that one affects the other. In fact, research has repeatedly shown that every aspect of our lives is connected. Behaviors and activities that take place in one "compartment" always affect what happens in other "compartments."

Compartmentalization can become a significant problem for church workers, as it can for everyone else. If all aspects of life connect, then church workers will find it helpful to think and behave more holistically, recognizing that every action has a systemic affect. The Wholeness Wheel is one helpful model.

The Worker Support Team (WST) had been formed over two years ago at St. Michael's. Lora, a social worker, and Ted, a chiropractor, were co-chairs, with Lora taking the lead by mutual consent for the group's latest initiative.

For months, the group had worked diligently to establish excellent relationships with each member of the St. Michael's staff. Together with the five members of the WST; Karen, the church secretary; Joyce, the director of Christian education (DCE); and Pastor Ken had talked about the Wholeness Wheel in a general way. The WST had asked each staff member to think about the

model and then to sit down individually with the WST, prepared to discuss it.

The members of the WST had all taken their tasks seriously. They had conscientiously completed the preliminary work described in previous chapters. Now, they were about to take the next step: individual conversations with each staff member. They scheduled an hour with each person and delegated two WST members—Lora and Ted—to conduct the conversations. That would help keep the discussion informal and, they hoped, helpful. (They planned to debrief at their next full meeting to make sure that was, indeed, what happened.)

First up was Pastor Ken. Lora and Ted welcomed him, and all three sat down around a circular table. All had copies of the Wholeness Wheel handout. Ted began with prayer: "Lord Jesus, You have promised that when two or three are gathered, You are in their midst. We are gathered in Your name, and we trust Your promise. Guide our thoughts, our words, and our actions that we might support one another as members of Your body. We pray especially for Pastor Ken, that our conversations might provide encouragement, support, and nourishment to him and to his ministry. Amen."

Lora then set out the goals for the meeting: "As we discussed at the meeting last month, we are going to be using the Wholeness Wheel to help with our conversation. We asked all staff members to consider the areas on the Wheel in terms of their own life and vocation here at St. Michael's. So what have you been thinking about, Pastor? How is the Wholeness Wheel rolling in your life?"

"Generally, I like where I'm at on a number of places on the Wheel," began Pastor Ken. "But I'd like to zero in on two parts. My wife had some thoughts on the physical well-being side of things because she thinks I don't get enough exercise—and she is right. So that's one piece of it that I'd like to talk about. Physically, I feel kind of sluggish and, at 46, I don't think that should be happening. The other area that challenged me is the slice labeled 'Intellectual Well-being.' "

"These are the two areas," Pastor Ken continued, "that are not rolling along as smoothly as I'd like."

"If I'm hearing this right, you're pretty satis-fied with most areas on the Wheel, but two of them might need some further attention," Lora reflected. "Will you tell us some more about the 'intellectual well-being' section?" Lora ques-tioned.

"Sure," replied Pastor Ken. "I don't see myself growing much intellectually. Come to think of it, I feel sluggish intellectually too. I do a good amount of Bible study in preparation for a sermon or a Bible class, and I learn through that process. But I think I may be missing something else."

"So your intellectual work and personal study are challenging, but it's not enough to fully satisfy you," noted Ted.

"Right," said Pastor Ken, surprised at the quickness and energy in his response.

All three fell silent for a moment while Pastor Ken thought about it for a few seconds. "I think part of what is missing is that I am doing just about all—well, actually 100 percent of my studying by myself. I wonder if I could use more of the kind of stimulation that comes from studying with others?"

"Let's work on that," said Lora.

What has happened at St. Michael's? The congregation has put in place a group of people charged with a focus on the health and well-being of the St. Michael's staff. That group has taken the time to identify what they want to accomplish. They have developed covenants to guide their behaviors, and they have established a set of strategies and tactics to achieve their goals. Above all, they have taken care to establish positive relationships between members of the WST and the staff. They have now adopted a tool, the Wholeness Wheel, to help them focus their work.

So far the conversation has identified two areas of concern for Pastor Ken—his physical and intellectual well-being.

"Have you thought about some intellectual well-being strategies?" asked Ted.

"I've started wondering about that," replied Pastor. "I'd like to investigate the doctor of ministry programs at a seminary. It would give me the chance to study with others, but it would also help me study topics that would support my ministry here at St. Michael's," replied Pastor Ken.

Lora had come prepared with a copy of St. Michael's budget. "There's not much here right now for continuing education," she said. "But if together we decide that this is the best way to address the need, the WST could ask the Finance Committee to build it into the budget for next year."

"I'll look around to find some possible programs and bring the ideas to the next meeting," offered Pastor Ken.

"Terrific!" said Lora and Ted almost simultaneously.

"What about the physical part?" asked Lora.

"I've never been one to work by myself to make major changes," replied the pastor. "It's kind of like the continuing education thing. A group encourages me to achieve what I set out to do."

Ted spoke up. "I have had contact with some fitness coaches. What if I can find someone to give us an initial hand?"

"That would be a great help," responded Pastor Ken.

By now, the hour was almost over. Laura summarized: "It looks like we have agreed that you, Pastor Ken, will investigate possible continuing education opportunities. You'll report back to us at our next meeting, and we'll work toward making something possible. We'll certainly advocate for you. And Ted, you will find fitness coaches who might help Pastor get started. If not in the next day or two, at least no later than our next WST meeting."

With three minutes remaining, Lora remembered that their covenant included a brief debriefing, so she asked Pastor Ken about his responses to the conversation.

"Frankly, I was a little anxious beforehand," he replied. "I've never done this before at any of the churches I've served, and while I knew we were working together, still I was wondering how open I could be about what I was thinking. But after we got started, I found it really helpful, especially in seeing how alike my struggles with intellectual stimulation and physical exercise are."

"I thought we worked together well," said Lora. Both Ted and Pastor Ken nodded. "I am really glad we could surface these things and, God willing, this will help us move forward to further support you, Pastor Ken. The way I see it, the people at St. Michael's really appreciate your leadership and your spiritual direction. If we can help to strengthen you, it really works to strengthen the whole congregation. Who knows what might come of it!"

> Lora asked Pastor Ken to close the conversation in prayer, which he did. As he left, he met Joyce, the DCE, waiting just outside the door, ready for her conversation with Lora and Ted.

What did St. Michael's Church do—specifically—to support their workers?

- Working through their governance process, St. Michael's added a Worker Support Team (WST) to their structure and charged the members of this team with concern for the health and well-being of their workers.

- They recruited members for this team, based on both expertise and a heartfelt concern for supporting the St. Michael's staff. Lora is a social worker and Ted, a chiropractor. The team also includes an HR professional, a nurse, and a public school teacher.

- Once formed, the WST took time to create and build relationships with one another and with staff members.

- They set up behavioral covenants and made promises focused on how they would do their work together.

- They found and used a resource to help guide the conversation with staff. Both WST members and staff studied the resource together.

- They scheduled and facilitated individual interviews.

- They guided staff to personalize specific plans to enhance well-being.

- They agreed to find resources to make the plans actionable.

Did you notice that the WST balanced two tasks as they talked with Pastor Ken? Completing the task at hand—the interviewing and planning—was important. But so was attending to the needs of each individual around the table. Lora and Ted worked together to make sure Pastor Ken knew they accurately heard what he was saying. Lora and Ted also monitored their relationship with Pastor Ken. Tasks and people both matter, and Lora and Ted understood this.

Lora and Ted worked to keep the setting comfortable and conducive to trust. They helped Pastor Ken clarify his thoughts. But they didn't just listen. They also suggested possible tactics. When resources were not immediately available, they began to develop a process to find them.

The meeting was sanctified by the Word of God and prayer, and the group debriefed as they had covenanted to do.

SPEAKING PERSONALLY

I've heard and participated in so many conversations that ended with either/or options. Such binary conversations usually end with one of two options: "The church worker needs to . . ." or "The congregation needs to . . ."

These binary options overlook an additional, essential option—the relationship option, the partnership. In this option, both the workers and the congregation work together to create solutions.

I have become convinced that the adversarial tone I hear so often flows from a breakdown in relationship. In such a context, people lay responsibility or blame on others. Then everyone begins to push, demand, and confront. This almost guarantees that a positive solution will not be found. Besides that, such behavior is not becoming to members of the Body of Christ.

As I consult with congregations and other groups, this principle seems very clear: conflict about issues such as compensation, continuing education, and workload are almost always fed by an underlying relationship breakdown. Participants could be fighting about almost anything. The real issue is the relationship. Thus, the forceful emphasis on partnering in this chapter.

Still, once formed, a strong partnership is not enough to address the well-being needs of staff. Good partners need good tools.

I helped develop the Wholeness Wheel, in part, to address that need for tools. Experts have developed many similar, secular wheels. In every case, they include a spiritual slice in the pie. But they do not center on Baptism as the core. For Christians, though, Baptism is the core event in life! It provides the center axis around which our lives turn.

We now turn to the specific slices of the Wholeness Wheel, the dimensions of life deeply influenced by the new identity God has given each of His children in Baptism.

CHAPTER ELEVEN

USING THE WHOLENESS WHEEL

A general who reinforces only one flank leaves troops elsewhere vulnerable to attack. The enemy will likely not attack the reinforced side of the battlefield. By strengthening that one area still further, he gains little tactical advantage. The enemy will attack at the weakest points, assuming he can find them. Continuing to reinforce just one or two areas of strength eventually weakens the chances of victory for all.

Similarly, having areas of significant vulnerability, weakness, or underdevelopment threatens the well-being of the entire person. An otherwise healthy employee who drinks to excess soon finds alcoholism affecting job performance. Eventually the person is fired, precipitating both financial and relationship crises. One area of weakness affects many others.

The Wholeness Wheel can help church workers identify areas of strength. It can also help discern areas of weakness. Then strategies for shoring up the weaknesses can be developed. It's vitally important, though, that workers feel safe enough to discuss areas of weakness honestly. Someone who feels under the proverbial gun won't likely speak with transparency or raise salient concerns.

Self-protection rather than helpful sharing will mark the process.

As conversations deepen, so likely will the need for problem solving at a deeper level, for deeper thought about appropriate strategies and tactics to address the concerns, issues, and frustrations that have been raised. This chapter illustrates that, but it only begins to tap the surface of what creative people, partnered together in service to one another in the Body of Christ and blessed by God's Holy Spirit, can develop.

EMOTIONAL WELL-BEING

Joy, irritation, closeness, sadness, jealousy, lust, anxiety, anger, panic, depression, exhilaration—human beings experience these emotions and dozens more besides. Everyone experiences emotions, even church workers. How our emotions are experienced and managed is key to effective living and service in Christ's Body.

> A few members at St. Michael's thought that Joyce was looking sadder and less energetic than usual. It was no surprise, then, that at the meeting with the Worker Support Team Joyce shared a dilemma. Over the past several months, she found herself more and more often caught between the needs of her immediate family (including her husband and 3 children, ages 16, 13, and 11) and her extended family (specifically, her aging parents who lived with ever-increasing health issues some 100 miles away).

Joyce freely admitted the strain was getting to her. It had also begun to affect her work. Her husband, Jim, was attentive and understanding. Still, he had started his own business two years earlier, and it zapped most of his energy and all of his time. Joyce also freely acknowledged that she set a high bar for herself professionally and now could not meet it. Lately, she had begun to think that she needed to resign her call at St. Michael's.

"I think we all can sense the struggle that you are experiencing," reflected Ted. "You're working to manage it, but it's no wonder your energy is gone. Before you decide to resign, though, would it be okay if we thought about some other options?"

Joyce agreed, and the group generated the following possibilities:

- Joyce could and likely should find a counselor. Most health insurance plans have a counseling option and sometimes an employee assistance program (EAP) as well. A small co-pay might be involved, but the help Joyce would receive in identifying and expressing her feelings would be invaluable. In addition, a counselor could also help her develop ways to attend to her feelings as she navigates some difficult terrain in the months ahead.

- Joyce could also ask Jim to accompany her to some counseling sessions. Again, the health insurance plan St. Michael's provides may help pay for it. Since Jim is clearly part of the solution and is certainly dealing with stressors himself, it would be helpful to the whole family if Joyce and Jim could work together on these troublesome concerns.

■ Joyce could consult with a social service agency that specializes in the needs of the elderly. An in-home evaluation of her parents' situation and the suggestions made by local experts could be very helpful.

■ Joyce could read any of several books on the "sandwich generation." Because Lora is a social worker, she will know about current titles and may even be able to loan copies to Joyce. In addition, Lora could offer to discuss the content informally with Joyce.

> Any and all of these ideas might help Joyce and Jim. Of course, the list is not exhaustive. Other options might surface in other communities or later on in this one. Regardless of St. Michael's location, though, members of the WST can help Joyce by recognizing the value of her work as the DCE at St. Michael's. They can express their thankfulness for her contributions in the past and commit to work with her during this time of special difficulty.

> What a blessing for Joyce (and for St. Michael's) that the congregation had an intentional and proactive support process in place. That process did not depend upon Joyce's coming forward. Instead, the WST met with Joyce as a matter of course. Her struggle was almost totally internal, but her conversation with the WST gave her the opportunity to share it with other members of the Body of Christ. This process of getting her emotions out of herself and onto the table was

critical for her—as it will be for every church worker from time to time over the course of a career.

PHYSICAL WELL-BEING

Physical well-being includes everything from blood pressure to cholesterol levels to weight control to exercise to nutrition to sleep patterns to sex to disease and disabilities. Each of us has a body, so each of us deals with issues of physical well-being. This includes church workers. For Christians, this is a stewardship issue. We care for our bodies as the gift from God that they are.

Pastor Ken focused, in part, on the issue of his physical well-being as he met with Lora and Ted. He described himself as feeling "physically sluggish," and he linked it to a pattern of trying to deal with his need for exercise by himself.

"I'm afraid if I make it a do-it-yourself project, I'll fail," he admitted. "I'll probably just drop out of the race, so to speak. I just don't have the staying power to stick with an exercise program."

"So you're seeing there is a need, but it doesn't have a high priority for you, especially if you have to motivate yourself all the time," Lora said, noting his ambivalence.

"On target," Pastor Ken responded. "I'll meet with the trainer Ted finds. But could we talk about how to stay motivated?"

As Pastor Ken contemplated making a lifestyle change, he wasn't sure about his level of commitment, but he was open to entertaining some options. Together, he, Ted, and Lora discussed the following—again, these are not exhaustive, but they are suggestive of creative approaches that might arise in such a conversation:

- To start, Pastor Ken should get a full physical and, in doing so, get his physician on board. If blood pressure or weight are issues of concern, this is especially important.

- Pastor Ken could commit to walking the stairs instead of taking the elevator whenever possible. This might be especially do-able in making hospital calls.

- He could also commit to parking as far as possible from the entrance to the hospitals, malls, and stores he visits.

- In general, Pastor Ken could commit to a general principle: intentionally looking for ways to work additional exercise into his natural activities, thus (literally) taking steps toward physical well-being.

- Pastor Ken could join a health club and get a fitness coach. Ted's contacts might be willing to work with the pastor on a regular basis in addition to setting up an initial program. The WST budget could have a small amount of money to support a membership fee.

- Perhaps Pastor Ken could put a note in St. Michael's weekly bulletin or monthly newsletter, asking if others might want to join him in his fitness endeavors. If so, this would create a natural support group.

As with Joyce in the illustration above, one of the most valuable aspects of the WST process for Pastor Ken was the members' expression of respect and support. Significantly, Lora and Ted also prayed with Pastor Ken, asking God to encourage the pastor in the changes he was making.

Intellectual Well-being

How does a congregation help their workers keep their intellects sharp? Generally, this involves a process of continuing education and a commitment by the worker to lifelong learning.

Many professions require continuing education. Many church vocations encourage it, but do not require it. For intellectual wellness, however, planning for continuous learning makes considerable sense.

For a few days after Pastor Ken talked with Lora and Ted about enrolling in a graduate program, he felt excited. As he reported the options he had discovered, though, he was more cautious. Where would the money for such a program come from?

Lora was determined to find a way to make it work.

"A couple of years ago," Pastor Ken said, "I tried to bring this up with the Board of Elders. They understood what I was saying, I think, but I was uncomfortable discussing it. I felt like I was tooting my own horn or being selfish, somehow. Now, I'm asking for the same thing, but it seems different. Maybe it's because the congregation has actually given you the task of helping me figure this out."

"I'm glad you feel comfortable with us," Lora answered. "Have you thought about what you might want to study?"

"As a matter of fact, I have," said Pastor Ken. And they were off and running.

With the help of members of the WST, Pastor Ken was able to put his concern into words. His current lack of intellectual stimulation had, for the moment, only marginal effects on his ministry. But the fact he was feeling "sluggish" suggests that the impact could become broader and more permanent if it is not addressed. How will he keep his intellect sharp? Together with Lora and Ted, he explored the following options:

- Pastor Ken could explore formal graduate programs and find a way to enroll in one.
- He could talk with other clergy in the area about the possibility of forming a study group focused on topics of mutual interest.
- He could read a book or two on adult learning with a view toward understanding the differences between the goals of informal adult learning and the goals of the traditional academy. Then he could use this information to set time-bounded goals for himself.
- Pastor Ken could sample an intensive two-week adult learning program on a topic of significant interest,

either locally or out-of-town. Alternatively, he could sample a continuing education event in a field quite different from his vocation and previous studies.

- He could begin to explore the possibility of a sabbatical, one which would allow extended time for full-time, focused study.

VOCATIONAL WELL-BEING

How is your job going? This is one of the essential questions raised by a discussion of the Wholeness Wheel. In addition, that Wheel raises broader questions of how work fits into a worker's sense of vocation, and whether or not the work is satisfying, rewarding, fulfilling, and seen as useful. Most research suggests that a major component of a satisfying work environment is good relationships with co-workers.

> Karen was somewhat apprehensive going into the WST's process. She had been the secretary at St. Michael's for eleven years now and had worked with two different pastors and three different DCEs. She really liked DCE Joyce and Pastor Ken, but she was concerned about how they viewed her. "No one has ever evaluated my performance," said Karen as she sat down to meet with Lora and Ted.

> "This isn't so much a performance review as it is a conversation about how we could work together to enrich your position and your enjoyment of it," replied Lora.

"But my performance is an important question for me," Karen said, with a force that surprised even her. "I do my job here, and I think I do it well, but I am not sure what other people think—other members of St. Michael's and also Pastor Ken and Joyce. And now you too!"

"When I thought about the Wholeness Wheel, I targeted 'Vocational Well-being,' because I think I am doing well, but I don't really know."

"It sounds as though you'd really like some feedback," reflected Lora, "maybe from members of St. Michael's, but especially from Pastor Ken and Joyce."

"Yes," said Karen, "and I also have some ideas about how we might make the office more efficient. Are you open to hearing them?"

"We'll certainly listen," said Ted, "but if we move into questions of equipment and supplies, we'll need to see who else we need to involve."

Clearly, Karen wanted feedback about her work. Clearly, she was not getting it. So far as Ted and Lora knew, there was no mechanism in place for such feedback. Now Karen had a voice, and almost immediately she was using it to improve office functionality. Together with Ted and Lora, she generated the following options:

- Karen could talk with Pastor Ken and Joyce about a regular employee review process. The WST might help facilitate that conversation. Such a process could help everyone could get feedback.

- Karen could ask the member of the WST with expertise in Human Resources to consult with the staff about developing the evaluation process.

- Karen could work with the WST to determine who would need to be involved in a discussion about office upgrades. Then she could help set up the discussion.

- Karen could research and evaluate a partnership with the Wellness Council of America (WELCOA, www .welcoa.org) to see if their Well Workplace application and awards would fit the small office at St. Michael's. After the research was complete, she could talk about it with Joyce and Pastor Ken, working to get their buy-in.

Again, this list is not exhaustive. Even so, it illustrates many facets of "vocational well-being." Workload, job description, staff relationships, staff-member relationships, job satisfaction, and the like are all potential discussion topics. This is why it is very useful to have someone with human resource experience serving on the WST. Not every congregation has such a person in its membership. The most important thing, however, is the process of getting things out on the table where they can be addressed in safe and respectful ways.

SOCIAL/INTERPERSONAL WELL-BEING

The capacity to positively engage other people in significant relationships is the central skill in "social/interpersonal well-being." People who work with people need strong social and interpersonal skills. Church workers who cultivate a vital and robust social and interpersonal life will be actively engaged with others in various contexts, not just the congregational context.

> Adrian was very excited when he first arrived at St. Paul's as the new director of Christian outreach (DCO). After many months, his excitement continued, but he also felt lonely. His new city was 400 miles from where most of his family lived. He loved his job, but other staff seemed somewhat distant. He hadn't yet built a reliable social network. As a result, he was starting to feel frustrated and a bit down. He was gaining weight because he was neither eating well nor exercising.
>
> At the end of his first year, when he sat down with his pastor to discuss his performance, a lot of his frustration and loneliness came out. St. Paul's was just forming a WST, so his pastor suggested asking two members of that group to join the discussion, even before the WST's first formal meeting.
>
> "I don't want this to be seen as a complaint against my job or the people at St. Paul's," Adrian began, "I'm just having difficulty establishing roots. And, as you know, there are not a whole lot of people my age at St. Paul's."
>
> The discussion lasted for two hours. Everyone really liked Adrian and wanted to help.

The group discussed the following options—again, these are suggestive, not exhaustive:

- The pastor and members of the WST could more actively ask Adrian about how he was doing and the staff could more intentionally include him in their discussions during the workday.

- Adrian could ask his local judicatory's office or ministerial association for the names of new church workers in the area. Adrian could then contact people making similar transitions.

- The pastor knew of one such person who had made a transition like Adrian's over the past two years and seemed now to be doing well. The pastor asked Adrian's permission to call this person and share Adrian's contact information.

- Adrian could contact larger area churches and the local YMCA to ask about two of his passions—softball and basketball. If leagues were forming soon, he could join. Although it might be difficult for Adrian to sign on to an existing team, the WST members encouraged him to do so if possible.

- Adrian could find a counselor with whom to share his transition issues. Having a safe person and the assurance of personal confidentiality might help speed the transition.

As in the other examples in this chapter, one of the most valuable things about Adrian's conversation with the pastor and WST members was the personal affirmation offered about Adrian and his work. Another most valuable aspect was the prayer offered and the promise of continuing prayer on his behalf. It also helped Adrian to get his feelings out on the table. He realized he'd been stewing about the issues for months, and all the inner turmoil had led him to withdraw from other staff members. Now, people were pulling with him and praying for him.

Among other things, this example makes it easy to see the interplay between one part of the Wheel and the rest of it. A holistic view is necessary as congregation members seek to support and care for their workers.

SPIRITUAL WELL-BEING

So far in this chapter, all of the clinical examples I have given involve a spiritual component. Every aspect of one's well-being is affected by one's spiritual well-being. That's why surrounding, and in some ways, holding the Wholeness Wheel together is the dynamic termed "spiritual well-being."

Church workers sap their strength in this regard more often than they realize. When one studies the Scripture and worships "professionally" week by week, it's easy to overlook a simple, but profoundly important question: How is your walk with Jesus going on a personal and experiential level?

This question does not claim that we do anything to merit God's grace, forgiveness, and love. Those are all gifts of God. Nor does it claim that we can measure the strength of someone's faith. God is at work in our lives, whether or not "I feel it."

Even so, a "professional" basis for faith erects barriers that can blunt the work of the Holy Spirit. For instance, church workers can objectify God's Word and Sacraments. So, for example, a pastor or DCO might study the Bible only in preparation for some vocational task. A pastor might listen to sermons by other pastors only for the purpose of critiquing the homiletical style. These things turn a personal relationship with God through Christ's redemptive work into just so much objective data. Thus, all church workers need a regular opportunity to explore their own spiritual lives. How is this done?

Congregations that understand this occupational hazard faced by its workers can offer the following encouragements—and perhaps more.

- Be in spiritual direction. In a regularly scheduled meeting each month, talk with a wiser and more spiritually mature person about your spiritual life. Have someone to whom you can confess your sins and receive Christ's absolution individually, a place where you can think through what God is teaching you, where you can receive prayer for specific concerns and concrete needs.

- Gather with peers for mutual sharing of self, life, relationships, and faith. If you include Bible study, be sure that part of the focus lies on direct application to life. It can happen among staff. But it also needs to happen apart from the congregation.

- Take periodic spiritual retreats. During your time away, read, meditate, receive counsel, and grow.

- Receive the Word and Sacrament often.

- If you are married, take a retreat with your spouse. Set aside regular time with your spouse every day for mutual sharing and prayer. Talk directly about the spiritual impacts of being a church worker and/or being married to a church worker.

■ If you are married, worship with your spouse. When you have opportunity to come together with other couples and families for worship and prayer, participate!

SPEAKING PERSONALLY

This chapter makes many specific recommendations for church worker care. Some occur more than once—seeking counseling, for example. As I've said throughout, these ideas are not meant to be an exhaustive list. Rather, I want to give readers a taste of what might emerge out of serious conversation in which congregational members and church workers engage deeply.

I also want readers to understand that church worker support includes much more than one appreciation day, week, or month each year, helpful as those events might be. Church worker support is a 24/7 journey in the lives of congregations and other Christian organizations.

I'm passionate about this because supportive relationships have literally saved my life. I have learned more than once that I do not effectively live life alone. Sometimes that realization has been painful; sometimes it has been simply refreshing and healing. Regardless, the reality is that like everyone else, I walk through life together with others, and those others are people whom Christ has placed in my life. They are His gifts.

As I finish this chapter, another important thought comes to mind. Perhaps it's occurred to you too. Supporting church workers is not a light or superficial task. It's serious business, taking time, energy, and prayer. We'll realize that even more as we consider the chapters ahead. I plan to sprinkle specific recommendations liberally throughout the remainder of the book. But they will not come as a list of to-dos. They will come, generally, in the context of life together in a vibrant, Christ-centered community.

We turn now to another set of tools designed to prevent burnout.

CHAPTER TWELVE

PREVENTING BURNOUT

Joan crossed paths with Phil as he came in to drop off a form at the school office. Phil and his wife, Cecilia, had one child at Concordia School. Phil had recently been elected to the school board. Joan had joined the Concordia faculty three years ago, immediately following her college graduation.

While it was not the most opportune time to launch a serious conversation, that morning Joan had pretty well had it. "Phil," she blurted out, "I need more support. I'm coming to the end of my rope." Tears welled up in her eyes.

Phil took her elbow and steered her out of the corridor and into the relative privacy of the library. "What's going on?" he asked.

"Teaching alone is no fun anymore," continued Joan.

"Support?" thought Phil. "It's a general term. What does she mean?" Then he spoke, "Joan, I can see you're really upset. I get that. I'm not sure what you mean by 'needing more support.' Can you clarify that?"

"Well it's just support," Joan retorted. "I just don't
have the support I need to do my work."

"Support" means different things to different people. In
the conversation between Joan and Phil, the word seems
to capture a series of unspecified disappointments and
concerns. Joan and Phil need to work together to clarify
these so they can move on to apply specific strategies.

Clarification is important on a number of levels. Most
obviously, it's hard to develop strategies to deal with something that is not fairly well-defined. Then, too, different
people can provide different kinds of support. To expect
one person to do it all will strain and overwhelm the relationship. Clarifying the different needs and then spreading
tasks out among several individuals tends to be healthier
and makes on-target support more likely. For instance,
Phil can help by listening to Joan, but if she needs to learn
better ways to manage a difficult class, Phil's expertise may
not apply. Joan may find an experienced teacher's mentor-
ing far more helpful.

Finally, when churches clarify needs, they can begin
to develop resources to address recurring problems. For
instance, St. John's Church has served a town of 5,000
people for more than a century. Its last two pastors had
come from cities with populations of over 100,000. Over
time, it has become obvious that St. John's needs an
intentional plan to help new workers learn how to navi-
gate small town culture. Recognizing this, congregational
leaders have asked the WST to find ways to translate small
town norms for the DCE who is about to begin her service
at St. John's.

Support systems are critical for everyone in every walk of life. This includes church workers. In this chapter I will discuss eight needs served by such support systems, applying each to life in congregations.

1. WHO SPEAKS TO ME OF GOD'S LOVE, ACCEPTANCE, AND FORGIVENESS THROUGH JESUS CHRIST?

In the Word preached and the Sacraments administered, all church workers receive God's love, acceptance, and forgiveness most assuredly and concretely. Church workers share all the characteristics of humankind: they are persons in need of a Savior with hearts in turmoil until they are found and given the peace that passes all understanding.

Church workers, as has been a theme of this book, sometimes do not place themselves in positions where the Spirit of God can move into their hearts. Some call this placing barriers in the way of the free action of the Holy Spirit. It is not necessarily done intentionally. Often it is just an occupational hazard of work in ministry.

Thus it is important, indeed vital and crucial, for church workers to have a place and space where their basic and core spiritual needs are addressed—directly, specifically, and concretely. Of all the support functions, the spiritual life and its support are most basic, the foundation on which all other support functions stand.

> It was not an easy thing for Pastor Rick to do. A fairly private man, in fact, a little introverted, he

generally kept things about himself to himself. But he was troubled. He approached another pastor and asked if the pastor would hear his confession. When the words "in the stead and by the command of my Lord Jesus Christ I forgive you all your sins in the name of the Father and of the Son and of the Holy Spirit" were spoken over him as his confessor also made the sign of the cross on his forehead, Pastor Rick bathed in the love, acceptance, and forgiveness that is his through Christ. Indeed, Christ for us, Christ for him!

An important emphasis made repeatedly in this book is that attention to this area of support of the church worker is crucial. Congregational leaders need not be shy in speaking of God's love and care directly to their workers.

2. WHO CHALLENGES ME IN MY SPIRITUAL WALK?

Not all paths are on smooth surfaces. As has been demonstrated throughout this discussion, church workers face significant challenges, one of which is that their walk with Christ may not be as alive and vibrant as it once was. It is not that Christ's love is less vibrant; it is that the worker of the Church is sensing less vibrancy in himself or herself.

Thus it is important for church workers to have people in their support systems that are ready and willing to challenge them spiritually.

"Got a moment?" said Sam to DCE Jenna. "Sure," she said. Sam explained, "I think I've noticed a lessening of your energy and excitement, and I'm wondering, first, if what I've noticed is actually on target and, second, if it is, how can I help?"

Jenna was stunned at first. "Fact is," she thought, "Sam is on target." The question in her mind was whether to talk to him about it or try to stonewall her way through it. Her relationship with Sam was quite good, having built over the several years he was on the Board of Parish Education.

"Let's sit down and talk about what you are seeing," Jenna finally replied. "Its funny—not in a 'ha ha' way, but in a strange way. Here I am doing church work in a church context and I'm not at all sure that my faith seems as alive as it once did."

This is spiritual challenge. Sam could, in a caring context and within a concerned relationship, raise with Jenna concerns about her that spoke directly to her spiritual walk. It is natural for congregation members to defer to church workers on these matters. Seeing them as the more or less experts in their field, they expect church workers to be on top of their own spiritual walk. In deferring they deprive the worker of this possible support need. Congregational leaders need not be shy in engaging their workers in this kind of a discussion or challenge.

3. WHO REALLY HEARS ME?

Everyone needs to vent sometimes. Everyone needs people who will listen without making judgments or giving advice. We all need to share our joys and successes as well as our pains, frustrations, and failures. We all need to let off steam. This is especially true for those who work with people, often in stressful circumstances.

Phil listened actively to Joan. He wanted to understand, not to judge or list a dozen solutions. Listening skills really are the foundation on which human relationships are built.

Where do church workers go when they need someone just to listen? Sometimes they vent spontaneously, without prior planning—as Joan did with Phil. These kinds of conversations go on every day on parking lots, in living rooms, and after church over coffee in the basement. In some ways, this kind of natural sharing is central to the life of the community formed by Christ.

Even so, serious concerns are best shared in private and with people sanctioned to help. Here are a few of many possible options:

■ Congregations could train listeners and assign them as the go-to persons for church workers who need to vent on a personal level. Most churches will need several listeners if their workers' need for support is to be well-satisfied. If a given staff member and listener do not connect in a natural, empathetic relationship, it is the responsibility of the congregation to appoint another listener.

■ Churches can encourage spiritual direction and counseling. In these one-on-one relationships, workers can lay on the table all their concerns and feelings.

Many church workers will feel more comfortable with a counselor who belongs to the American Association of Pastoral Counselors (www.aapc.org) or with a Christian member of another professional counseling association.

■ As new leaders are oriented, the church may want to provide an in-service event focused on group leadership and listening skills. In this way, the congregation recognizes the need for staff support and intentionally plans for it by training its leaders in it. The benefits go far beyond staff support too. Leaders with this kind of training can facilitate meetings in such a way that everyone present has a voice and is heard.

1. Some congregations take a yearly retreat that includes staff and lay leadership—even if the "staff" is only one person. They spend a half-day together, reviewing the year past, planning for the year ahead, and listening to each other on a personal level. It's best if someone outside the congregation facilitates. It's even better if the facilitator has professional team-building experience.

2. Churches can support their workers in attending teachers' conferences, pastoral conferences, DCE conferences, and the like. When ministry peers come together, a lot of listening goes on.

4. WHO HELPS ME SEE WHAT IS?

There are two kinds of reality: physical reality and social reality. Physical reality makes it prudent to use an umbrella or raincoat in a downpour. Social reality isn't always so obvious. Sometimes it takes a friend to help us interpret social reality and think through how to act appropriately.

> Pastor Jim came from an expressive family. A pat on the back, an arm around the shoulder, a high-five—all communicate friendship and affection for Pastor Jim and his family members.
>
> As Pastor Jim arrived at his first church, he was excited to get going in ministry and every facet of his extroverted spirit showed this. His parishioners, however, came from older European stock. They greeted him politely, but with restraint.
>
> After a few months, this began to disturb the new pastor. "Maybe they don't like me," he thought to himself.
>
> One day, Pastor Jim called on Mary, a 92-year-old shut-in. Somehow, the conversation turned to the members' response. "From all I hear, people love you," said Mary.
>
> "But they don't seem to show it," said Pastor Jim.
>
> Mary smiled, then spoke from her many years of wisdom. "They don't show it the way you show it, but they feel it. Besides, if they didn't like you, you'd know about that!"

Mary helped Pastor Jim do some reality testing. He had one emerging interpretation of what he was seeing and experiencing. He based his interpretation on his own family-of-origin and their way of dealing with relationships. But the culture in his new church differed. Pastor Jim needed an interpreter; Mary stepped up to make the translation. Over time, Pastor Jim found her an invaluable translator of congregational culture and custom.

Pastor Jim found Mary. Mary was an able translator, but it does not always work that way. Ideally, a congregation will take steps to help their workers understand its culture. Here are a few possibilities:

- When a new worker enters the community, a congregation could assign several people to orient him or her. These volunteers should help the worker meet people in the community; they should also take time to discuss local customs and history.

- Churches might identify people like Mary in the story above—wise, mature Christians within the congregation who can serve as social reality testing coaches. As new workers explore new relationships, places, and culture, the coaches can help interpret the worker's observations.

- Congregations might also identify spiritually mature young adults and high school students, asking them to interpret their culture for new workers. The culture of these groups may differ from that of the adults.

- Churches can set up more formal structures (e.g., a WST) to manage this need. Members of such groups can open conversations on either side of the social reality testing equation. The WST is charged with keeping an ear to the ground, and can raise social reality concerns about which the worker may not be aware.

5. WHO IS SIDE-BY-SIDE
WITH ME REGARDLESS?

Supporting a worker emotionally involves being by their side as they go through difficulties, even when we don't totally agree with their actions or attitudes. Most of us need at least one ally in hard times. Many of us would benefit by having four or five such allies. Even when someone has behaved badly, he or she still needs someone to rely on, someone who won't run at the first or second or third sign of trouble. Church workers need this too.

> Deaconess Jena was mortified. She had lost her temper during a Worker Support Team meeting when someone criticized her work ethic. "What did people think?" she thought. "But even more, what do I think of myself? I didn't recognize myself! I feel rotten."

> Even after Jena apologized to the group and they offered their forgiveness, the fallout continued. Georgia, a member of the congregation's WST, followed Deaconess Jena down the hall after the meeting. She put her arm on Deaconess Jena's shoulder and said, "That was rough. But remember, you're still the talented and gifted person God has made you in Christ. If you'd like to talk some more about what happened, I'm open to that."

This kind of emotional support is not easily built into a congregation's life. A few people will stand by church workers regardless of their behavior. While helpful, that tendency does pose a danger in that members may start to choose up sides, for and against the worker. While emotional support is essential, it's equally important to make sure to support the worker, but not the bad behavior. Georgia, for example, came to the side of Deaconess Jena without excusing her outburst. This is a variant of the adage, "We love the sinner and hate the sin."

Here are a few ways congregations can provide intentional support of this kind:

- Congregations can celebrate confession and forgiveness in ways that run deeper than mere outward piety. It needs to become a central way-of-being among members of the congregation. In this kind of a culture, people can and do step forward to support others, realizing they are all equally bereft of merit apart from Christ.

- Churches can encourage their workers to find a confessor to whom they take specific sins, name them, confess them, and then hear the wonderful words of absolution.

- All churches can develop policies and encourage attitudes that strengthen the marriages of their workers. Those workers who enjoy strong, healthy marriage relationships can receive genuine emotional support from their spouses. Thus, churches should provide time, money, childcare, and other supports needed so that workers can attend marriage enrichment events.

- All churches can develop policies and encourage attitudes that strengthen the relationships of church workers with one another. Strong, supportive peer relationships can provide deep emotional support. Attendance at peer conferences should be encouraged and supported financially whenever possible.

■ Congregations can encourage and support the use of counseling resources. I've mentioned this before and will mention it again. In times of care and stress, there's often no substitute for having a counselor standing alongside the church worker, supporting and challenging in ways others simply cannot.

6. WHO WILL CHALLENGE ME: MY THOUGHTS, FEELINGS, AND BEHAVIORS?

It's easy to convince ourselves that we're doing our best when we aren't. It's comforting to think we've done all we can do when we haven't. Sometimes, it's easier to blame others for our problems, rather than taking responsibility for our own actions. Defense mechanisms can be helpful on occasion, but when overused they block emotional growth and damage relationships.

> Deaconess Jena was still angry over the exchange at the WST meeting. "What right did Laura have to critique my work ethic?" Jena thought, fuming. "I'm the one who is theologically trained, and I need time to study. How dare she say she thinks I spend too much time in my office? I have every right to be angry with her. She is just ill-informed and insensitive."

> Georgia, a member of the WST and Jena's friend, put her arm around Jena's shoulder after the

> meeting. "That was rough," she said, "But after you have a chance to cool off a bit, I'd like to talk further with you about it. I think there may be some things you are not seeing clearly. I like you, and I care about you. You're very gifted. But your feelings need some attention."

Responding to some personal challenges is a more difficult, but necessary part of the support church workers need. Accountability for behavior and a feedback process that allows and encourages accountability is crucial. It can't happen, though, outside a relationship anchored in trust.

Had Deaconess Jena's critic been the one to follow her down the hall and challenge her still further, the exchange would not have gone well. The trust factor would be missing. Georgia could talk with Jena, though, because the two had a positive, pre-existing relationship, one that could withstand the challenge.

Informal relationships aside, what processes can congregations use when emotional difficulties arise? In addition to those listed above, here are a few more ideas:

- Find ongoing ways to cultivate trust between church workers and members of the WST. Trying to build trust when conflicts have already arisen will doom you to failure. Take time before storms brew to develop safe, trusting relationships.

- Develop policies and practices that strengthen the relationships of church workers with one another. Peers can sometimes challenge one another in ways that congregational members can't.

- Again, I can't encourage and support the use of professional counseling resources enough. Counselors have a responsibility to challenge their clients in a context of care and concern. They can say things and suggest things friends and peers usually cannot.

7. WHO TELLS ME I'M DOING GOOD WORK?

"Technical appreciation" is not a common term, but it is a helpful one. It refers to the acknowledgement and affirmation of someone's work by others who have the specific skills, understandings, and integrity to evaluate that work.

It is one thing if Joe praises Angela for the progress his son is making in Angela's classroom. This is part of the general culture of appreciation discussed in chapter 6. It is something else entirely if Joe is a teacher himself and praises Angela for her up-to-date teaching methods. Both are meaningful statements of appreciation, but each carries a somewhat different meaning.

> Pastor Ryan got lots of positive feedback, most of it coming after each church service. As he greeted people, folks would generally say something like, "Thank you for your encouraging words" or "Great sermon, pastor!" or "Your sermon made me think this morning" or "You touched my heart today." Every once in a while, someone would question something he had said or even tell him that his sermon missed the mark. But by and large, his hearers responded positively.

> Still, sometimes he wondered, "If my seminary professor heard my sermon, what would be the reaction?" He even mused, "Would other pastors think I'm doing a good job?" The only pastor in his congregation, Pastor Ryan would shrug and conclude, "I guess I'll just have to keep on wondering about that."

What was Pastor Ryan missing? The possible positive evaluation of his professional work by experts in his field. How might a congregation help with this area of social support? Some of these ideas will have a familiar ring by now.

■ Establish a congregational culture that supports life-long learning and growth. When the whole church wants to keep on learning, the church workers will usually be caught up in the flow. Part of such a culture always includes making resources (time and money) available to support opportunities for ongoing education.

■ Survey members of the congregation to learn about members who work in vocations that parallel the work of the church staff. Bring a small group of those people together to provide consultation and support. For instance, teachers in nearby public or private schools could form a support group for teachers in the congregation's school or for the pastor's confirmation instruction. Social workers who serve an aging population could form a support group for a deaconess or pastor who makes many calls on shut-ins.

- Develop policies and processes that strengthen the relationships of church workers with one another. In a supportive culture, peers can encourage one another professionally as well as personally. Professional conferences are especially important in this regard, especially when staff members have an opportunity to demonstrate their own work, not just listen to someone else talk about theirs.

- Offer church workers the opportunity to be coached. Coaching is often done through telephone conference calls as well as face-to-face. For instance, a pastor who wishes to improve his group meeting skills could hire a coach to work with him specifically around the development of that skill.

8. WHO WILL CHALLENGE MY WORK SO THAT I CAN GROW?

In many churches, the staff consists of only one or two people. By virtue of their position, these workers are the undisputed experts. Few members will challenge their expertise. In times of stress, that can feel quite comforting. If it goes on too long, though, it can contribute to burnout.

When we aren't challenged, we may find ourselves feeling bored and stagnant. On the other hand, there's a fine line between challenge and defiance. Church workers can benefit from being challenged, but few members will willingly take on this task. Nor are many truly qualified to do so. Helpful challengers must have enough genuine expertise to be able to identify areas for improvement. In addition, they must be trustworthy. If they approach the task to humiliate the worker or to enhance their own egos, they can cause great harm.

If no one challenges church workers, how will they improve? Appreciation and challenge are two sides of the same coin. Appreciation is expressed when a job is done well; challenges are raised when there's room for improvement. As in many other instances, a prior relationship of trust and respect is crucial. All of us find welcoming challenges difficult, even church workers. How much more so if the challenge is embedded in a distant or hostile relationship or if it comes from someone who may not have the expertise to raise the issue.

> Pastor Ryan had begun to get mixed feedback after church several weeks in a row. People who usually beamed said simply, "Good morning, pastor" or "Great singing today, pastor!" or "Are you not feeling well? You seem so tired." By and large, the members' responses were, well, flat.
>
> Pastor Ryan wondered, "How am I doing, anyway? How could I figure it out?"

The dissatisfaction Pastor Ryan senses from his members has left him feeling somewhat vulnerable. He could easily get defensive if someone approached him. Aware of this, how might his church support him? Here are a few possibilities:

- Because the WST has the responsibility to gather congregational feedback, they can legitimately engage this kind of a concern and bring it to the worker. As

I have said many times already, it's crucial that a pre-existing climate of trust between the worker and the WST be developed early and cultivated continually.

- Churches that create a culture of continual learning and growth will already have in place specific opportunities for continuing education. Workers in churches like that can comfortably engage those opportunities.

- With the full consent and blessing of the church worker, look for members whose vocations parallel that of the worker who needs help. Gather a small group of those people together to provide consultation and support for the worker. If the worker seems reluctant, the process will likely not produce the desired results, so work toward true consensus.

- Offer workers opportunities for coaching. As I said above, coaching often happens by phone from a distance. For instance, a pastor who wishes to improve his preaching skills could hire a coach—perhaps a seminary professor whom he knows and respects—to work with him to develop that specific skill more fully.

SPEAKING PERSONALLY

In my own life I have echoed a considerable amount of the anguish that is expressed by fictional teacher Joan. I get a general sense that I need something that I label as "support," but then have some difficulty identifying what that support might be. It has been a necessary and helpful thing to begin to identify those support needs and give them voice.

When I was called to serve at the national offices of The Lutheran Church—Missouri Synod, I clearly had a sense that I needed some support in something or other, despite the fact that folks were welcoming, hospitable, and really engaged in being "supportive." What I discovered I needed, among other things, was in the area of "Who Tells Me I'm Doing Good Work?" and "Who Will Challenge My Work so that I Can Grow?" sections from above. I discovered the Professional Church Leadership group, who were people who were doing things like I was doing in their own denominations. This discovery was wonderful! Here were people that were not only my professional peers, but they were in similar administrative positions. I learned and grew very much there.

It was also during this time that I discovered the Pines and Aronson resource, *Career Burnout: Causes and Cures*. My thinking in this area has been greatly influenced by them, and this chapter and the one following carry some echoes of their work. I highly recommend their book.

I also learned that I am a little (or maybe a lot) anxious about professional feedback. In short, I struggle to constructively receive challenges. I like to believe I do pretty good work. For instance, if a reviewer pans this book I think I will feel hurt, at least at first. But I continue to learn to grow from challenges. I also have learned that those challenges are best received when they come in a context of a trusting relationship, something I might not have with a negative reviewer I do not know. Ah, a growth point.

I have also learned that I tend to shy away from positive feedback. It is an interesting ambiguity. I kind of "aw shucks" this. But this, too, has inhibited my growth at times because it gets in the way of realistically assessing strengths and using them. It also gets in the way of offering heartfelt praise to the author of all gifts.

The focusing of areas that are needed for "support" is, I believe, very important. Congregational leadership needs to help church workers move from generic concerns to a more specific identification of that which is needed. It is to this task that we next turn.

CHAPTER THIRTEEN

USING SOCIAL SUPPORT FUNCTIONS

J. L. Moreno, the noted psychiatrist who founded a school of counseling called psychodrama, asserted that the human being is never totally reducible just to himself or herself. There is a community that surrounds that person. Moreno called this community the person's social atom. Surrounding the person are numbers of people who fulfill significant needs.

Chapter 12 described what some have called "social support functions." These are not the only support functions, but they are significant ones. Church workers will need some support in all these areas. But the support that is needed is not equal for all and also changes from time to time. Church workers need support in all areas. They need people who will (1) speak to them of God's love, acceptance, and forgiveness through Jesus Christ; (2) challenge them in their spiritual walk; (3) genuinely and deeply hear and understand them; (4) help them see what the reality of things actually is; (5) be emotionally side-by-side with them; (6) engage and even confront them as to their thoughts, feelings, and behaviors; (7) tell them they are doing good work; and (8) engage and even confront them as to the quality and appropriateness of their work.

The Worker Support Team (WST) at St. Timothy has worked together with staff for several years. It's hard to imagine stronger relationships. In a month, a new teacher will be joining pastors Josh and Clint, DCE Linda, principal Kathy, teachers Melinda, Scott, Ruth, Eve, Melissa, and Anthony, parish administrative assistant Laura, and school secretary Wanda on the staff.

St. Timothy is blessed with an incredibly gifted membership and has been able to include many as WST members. Robert, a fitness coach and physical therapist, chairs St. Timothy's WST. John and Lisa, teachers in a local public school, serve with Robert, as does Sandra, a psychologist. Maryanne, a human resources consultant; Samuel, a small business owner; Joel, a dentist; and Melissa, a stay-at-home mom, round out the team.

Sandra and Maryanne understand the importance of covering all six social support bases as a way of preventing burnout. They want to help the entire WST buy in and use the model to support the workers at St. Timothy.

"I have a list of eight support functions that I'd like to use. A lot of this thinking comes out of secular approaches to stress and burnout, but I think it could help us help our staff in valuable ways," Sandra began.

Pastor Clint agreed. "God gives us many gifts in the creation. We confess that in the First Article of the Apostles' and Nicene Creeds. If this has a basis in the behavioral sciences, and if the research backs it up, I think we ought to use it and see if it helps. I'd be willing to go first."

"Perhaps we could all study it a little more and then decide what direction to take," offered Robert. Sandra distributed copies of the social support functions worksheet.

HOW ARE MY SUPPORT NEEDS BEING MET?

There is an old adage that no one is an island. This is especially true of people who have been brought together by Christ into His Body, the community of people who follow Him. This worksheet identifies eight support needs.

TASK ONE: How important are these support needs to you at this time? All are likely important, but some may be more important to you than others at this time. Use a five-point scale, with **5** being very important, **1** being not very important, and **3** being a middle point.

To have people speak to me of God's love, acceptance, and forgiveness

          1   2   3   4   5

WORKSHEET

WORKSHEET

To have people challenge me in my spiritual walk

1 2 3 4 5

To have people genuinely and deeply hear and understand me

1 2 3 4 5

To have people help me see the reality of things or reality-test

1 2 3 4 5

To have people walk emotionally side-by-side with me without judgment

1 2 3 4 5

To have people confront or challenge me as to my thoughts, feelings, and behavior

1 2 3 4 5

To have people communicate to me that I am doing good work

1 2 3 4 5

To have people confront or challenge me concerning the quality of my work

TASK TWO: How well are these support needs being met at this time? Use a five-point scale, with **5** being very well, **1** being not well at all, and **3** being a middle point.

To have people speak to me of God's love, acceptance, and forgiveness

    1   2   3   4   5

To have people challenge me in my spiritual walk

    1   2   3   4   5

To have people genuinely and deeply hear and understand me

    1   2   3   4   5

To have people help me see the reality of things or reality-test

    1   2   3   4   5

To have people walk emotionally side-by-side with me without judgment

    1   2   3   4   5

To have people confront or challenge me as to my thoughts, feelings, and behavior

    1   2   3   4   5

To have people communicate to me that I am doing good work

    1   2   3   4   5

To have people confront or challenge me concerning the quality of my work

    1   2   3   4   5

TASK THREE: Check those support needs above that have a high level of importance and a high level of being met. These are areas of nourishment and growth for you. Strategies can be developed to keep these areas strong. Note these areas in the space below.

_____

_____

_____

_____

TASK FOUR: Circle those support needs above that have a high level of importance but a significantly lower level of being met. These are areas of increased vulnerability and may leave you more prone to vocational struggle. Strategies can be developed to strengthen these areas. Note these areas in the space below.

_____

_____

_____

_____

TASK FIVE: Look again at the noted areas in Tasks Four and Five. List the names of those who could help you meet your needs. Some names may appear several times. Rejoice, and continue to strengthen those relationships. At the same time, consider that names appearing many times may indicate an overloaded relationship, and a wise course of actions is to develop other relationships that will meet these needs.

_____

_____

_____

_____

"Could each of us fill it out on our own? Then we could talk about it, sharing what we each want to share?" asked Sandra. Robert was encouraged by this, but he wanted to make sure everyone understood the task. "We'll all do it," he clarified, "And we'll share. But we also want to keep our focus. How can we use this to help support our staff?"

"The first step," Sandra pointed out, "is to look at the eight support needs and give each a rating on a scale of 1 to 5 as noted."

If you and your church decide to use this instrument, that process will be your first step too. Each function is important to some degree, but they will vary in importance from person to person and from church to church. Completing this inventory helps each staff person begin to identify the most important support areas for him or herself. The higher the number, the more important that support need is for that person. The support needs staff identify as most important call for special attention. If they are not covered well, the lack of support in that area will create important vulnerabilities—in the life of the worker and among the people served by that worker.

> After everyone had finished, Sandra continued, "The next step is to think about how each need or function is being met. Use the number rating to establish how well it is being met. This will take a little time, so don't rush."

This second step draws each participant more deeply into an examination of the support needs and how well they are fulfilled in his or her own life. Optimally, the most important functions (identified in Task One) are well-satisfied (rated in Task Two). A function that is well-satisfied would receive a rating in the range from 4 to 5. When the most important functions receive scores of 1 or 2, it indicates a vulnerability that should be addressed.

> When everyone had finished, Brenda asked, "Who's willing to share something they wrote down?"

> Pastor Clint jumped in. "To have people challenge me in my spiritual walk was an idea that caught me off-guard. I really haven't thought about that as particularly important, but I know that I don't have many people, even my fellow pastors, who come up to me, look me in the eye, and ask how my spiritual warfare is going. This is going to need some work, though I think I can ask a close friend of mine to help me with this. Still, it is an open question how you can help me here." "Maybe we should just ask you from time to time," suggested Anthony. "Maybe so," responded Pastor Clint.

> "Otherwise," continued Pastor Clint, "the most important needs for me were 'to have people

genuinely and deeply hear and understand me' and 'to have people confront or challenge me concerning the quality of my work'. I have only one person, Pastor Josh, in that area, and the coverage of that need is a bit thin. When we talk with each other, we do critique what we are doing, but this is a large parish. We're busy and we don't get to talk one-on-one about professional issues too often."

"That's really interesting," chimed in Pastor Josh. "I rated the same way, both as to importance and coverage. Maybe great minds really do run along the same paths. We've never talked about this need in a focused way. Maybe we need to schedule a regular time to share what we are doing and get feedback from each other."

"I'd like that," said Pastor Clint quickly. "This is a great opportunity to learn and grow together," he thought.

Chairman Robert asked, "And you will get back to the WST to report on how your plan is working?"

"Absolutely," promised both pastors, almost simultaneously.

This episode illustrates one advantage of direct conversation in a safe space using a tool like the Support Needs Worksheet. Two staff members at St. Timothy are now working together to develop more coverage of the support needs that are important to both of them. Still, neither this discussion nor their action plan marked the end of the process. Accountability and follow-up also are necessary. Robert made sure an accountability piece was also added. Not only would the two pastors meet to work up a schedule, they would also tell the WST what they had done.

Over the next forty-five minutes or so, others shared their thoughts. Toward the end of this highly energized meeting, Robert wondered aloud, "This has obviously been an important way to talk about things that really matter in our lives. But we need to keep the momentum going. We need to plan our next steps. How will we do this?"

Principal Kathy was the first to respond. "I'd like to see us use the instrument in a couple of ways. First, I think it would be good if at our next faculty meeting, we talked about our results together as a faculty. In addition, we have David coming on board. He hasn't been in on this conversation, but I think he ought to have the opportunity to work through the exercise, even though he might not have many areas covered early on. I don't want to legislate this, though. If other faculty members don't think it's a good idea, let's drop it."

Faculty heads nodded enthusiastically around the table. Sandra spoke up. "This makes sense as a next step," she agreed.

"The second thing I'd like to see," Kathy continued, "is for us as a group—the faculty or all of us here today, or each of us individually, to sit down with members of the WST to talk about what has to happen so we can address our most important functions."

"I agree," said Pastor Josh. At least Pastor Clint, Linda, and I ought to meet. Or as you suggest, Kathy, we could all meet together."

"What about Wanda and me?" asked Laura, the parish administrative assistant. "Where do we fit in?"

"Maybe you could meet with the church staff at first," said Pastor Josh, "and Wanda can meet with the school staff. Then we'll see where to go from there."

"Don't leave us out," Samuel chimed in. "Now that we have learned to use the tool, it would be good for all of us on the WST to talk over what we've learned."

"Tell you what," said Robert. "I suggest the church staff, school staff, and WST members each meet separately, and then we'll all come back together to decide on next steps. We can all report on what we have discovered and what plans we have made for addressing needs. Then, at some point, I think it would be good if each member of the St. Timothy staff met with a couple of members of the WST to make specific plans, to the extent that we can do so. But let's talk about if that makes sense and seems useful at our next meeting."

Everyone agreed and Robert asked, "Pastor Josh, will you please close our meeting in prayer?"

"I'd love to," said Pastor Josh.

Many important things happened during this session. The Support Needs Worksheet focused discussion. Each member of the group invested considerable energy in filling it out and then shared energetically. Their personal investment helped everyone feel excited about sharing what each had learned. God's Holy Spirit certainly blessed the group with joy, charity, and unity of purpose as they built on strong, pre-existing relationships.

The plans for accountability and follow-up were especially important. Oftentimes, after energetic conversation, nothing happens. Identifying and committing to next steps will keep the momentum rolling.

This is one example of how churches can use this tool. In this case, the doing and sharing was planned and next steps emerged out of the group process. In the previous example, the Wholeness Wheel in chapter 10, the doing and sharing formed part of a fully planned process that included one-on-one interviews. The Wholeness Wheel could be used in a group process, and the Support Needs Worksheet could be used with individual members of the church staff. Whatever approach your church takes, remember that the important features of any process include the following:

1. Groups that gather in the church gather around the cross of Christ; it is Christ who brings His people together.

2. Relationships of trust and safety need to be built and constantly reinforced.

3. Group members need to listen to the personal stories and viewpoints of each participant.

4. Using tools such as the Wholeness Wheel or the Support Needs Worksheet will help focus the discussion.

5. Participants should be encouraged, but not forced, to share.

6. Specific strategies and tactics need to be developed, based on what is learned.

7. Plans for accountability and follow-up are essential.

8. Follow-up must actually happen.

9. Meetings are begun, continued, and ended in prayer.

SPEAKING PERSONALLY

Throughout life, I have found processes that help me focus on specific outcomes quite helpful. This is one reason I have included the Wholeness Wheel and the Support Needs Worksheet in this book. I tend to think more in generalities. It is easy for me to get caught up in the big picture and never get around to creating specific solutions to specific problems. When I focus, though, I can begin to plan.

I have also found an understanding of life together in

the Body of Christ compelling. Christ forms the Church. This is theological reality. It goes against my "pull yourself up by your bootstraps" mentality, but the fact is, I need to be in community to grow. The fact is, I need the community of Christ to help me focus. The fact is, Christ has called me to community with others in His Body through my Baptism.

As I wrote about the Support Needs Worksheet for this chapter, I became much more aware of one of my own social support needs—the need for people who still confront or challenge me concerning the quality of my work and/or communicate to me that I am doing good work. I currently teach at a seminary, but the only feedback I get comes from my students. Their feedback is important, of course. Still, I have never asked another instructor to observe and critique me, and I certainly have not asked a trained educator to do so. Furthermore, our faculty seldom talks about teaching methods. In short, this is a pretty vulnerable area for me. Hmm! It's likely time to create some strategies to deal with this! Perhaps I can ask my colleagues in education to observe my class and give me feedback.

CHAPTER FOURTEEN

SPIRITUAL WARFARE
AND CHURCH WORKERS

Finally, be strong in the Lord and in the strength of His might. Put on the whole armor of God, that you may be able to stand against the schemes of the devil. . . . Stand therefore, having fastened on the belt of truth, and having put on the breastplate of righteousness, and, as shoes for your feet, having put on the readiness given by the gospel of peace. In all circumstances take up the shield of faith, with which you can extinguish all the flaming darts of the evil one; and take the helmet of salvation, and the sword of the Spirit, which is the word of God, praying at all times in the Spirit, with all prayer and supplication. To that end keep alert with all perseverance, making supplication for all the saints, and also for me, that words may be given to me in opening my mouth boldly to proclaim the mystery of the gospel, for which I am an ambassador in chains, that I may declare it boldly, as I ought to speak. (Ephesians 6:10–11, 14–20)

In this chapter, we return to some of the ideas from chapter 1 and to the brief discussion about "spiritual well-being" that became part of the Wholeness Wheel conversation in chapter 11. As noted in those places, when church workers actively connect the Gospel of Jesus Christ to the real-life experiences of people, they will encounter frequent attacks. They will experience "the devil's schemes" and "the flaming arrows of the evil one." Those we serve want us to connect the Gospel with their daily lives. They deeply yearn for it, though ambivalently at times.

Church workers who keep their teaching and counsel theoretical will likely not experience as many direct threats. These include church workers who deliver lectures about God in sermons and classrooms, and who make academic or ritualized individual visits. When we fail to focus on where people are at, we stir up less of hell's animosity. Likewise, church workers will be less of a target when they abandon or downplay the Word of God and offer remedies drawn only from psychological, sociological, or other human sciences.

However, the more a worker seeks to help people connect their daily lives and experiences with the Gospel, and the more a congregation or school encourages members to make those connections, the more danger that worker, that school, and that congregation are in.

Many books written primarily to church workers focus on the worker's responsibility to be as healthy as possible in terms of attention to personal attitudes and behaviors. Books like these point the church worker to the importance of behavior patterns that are health-oriented and spiritually sustaining. What is a bit less clear, though, is how congregations can go beyond just encouraging to being actively helpful. This is especially important with regard to spiritually healthful behaviors.

Encouraging church workers to foster their spiritual well-being is, of course, very important. But such encouragement has potentially at least two negative effects. First, it places total responsibility on the worker, failing to involve the Body of Christ in effective and sustaining ways. Second, if the congregation does not have in place supportive policies and a supportive culture, encouragements alone won't be enough. In fact, they can have the opposite effect, putting workers into a situation in which they are encouraged and expected to care for their own spiritual health, but must violate congregational policies or expectations in doing so.

For instance, if a congregation encourages its pastor to meet with peers for Bible study, prayer, and conversation, but then objects when he is out of the office each week for such meetings, what is he to do? If the meetings take place at some distance and the congregation does not reimburse him for his mileage, the policy and expectations are at cross purposes. The net result is likely that the pastor strongly wishes to attend, but actually attends less and less often. Thus, his support system is weakened and part of the spiritual armor described in Ephesians 6 is lost.

Congregational policies must match congregational understandings of the spiritual danger in which they place their workers. Congregations need to encourage their workers, and they must help facilitate healthful worker behaviors.

Similarly, one occupational hazard of serving professionally in the church is a growing resistance to the penetration of the Word of God in the heart and soul of the worker. This resistance is built over time by familiarity with the Scriptures and church doctrine and by using these things "professionally." The very thing that gives life, a gift of God, is blocked by this hardness. What is the worker to do then? How can the church or school help?

SPIRITUAL ADVISING/ COUNSELING/DIRECTION

Leo has been a DCE at St. Andrew's for eleven years. This church was his first assignment. By all accounts, Leo has done exceptional work. The youth, young adult, and adult education programs have all grown in numbers and in depth of instruction. Leo has great relationships with almost all members of the congregation, especially the under-35 crowd. He is seen as energetic, committed, passionate, and dedicated. The changes in Leo are not yet easy to see, but there are changes. On the outside, Leo still pushes to be the kind of person that he, as he would say, "was." But on the inside, a wall is growing.

At first, Leo just sensed the change. "Something just wasn't the same," he says. Then the change became more noticeable. "It's my heart," he said to Faith, his wife. "My heart feels like it is dying. I don't feel a passion for the faith. I don't feel close to Jesus anymore. It's like there's a chasm between God and me." Alarmed, Faith encouraged Leo to spend more time in Bible study at home and in his office.

"I've tried that," Leo replied, "I just sit and read the Bible but . . . I can't really explain it—it's just not getting through."

"Well, what about talking to someone other than me about this?" Faith suggested.

"Like who?" asked Leo.

"How about Pastor Jake?" (Pastor Jake, recently retired from the congregation, still lived in the area. He had mentored Leo during Leo's first few years at St. Andrew's. Their relationship had always been positive.)

"That might work as a first step for me. I'm not struggling with anything in my job itself. It's my spiritual life, and maybe Pastor Jake could be my spiritual advisor."

"Besides," Faith reminded Leo, "St. Andrew's has always stressed that everybody on staff needs to have someone they can talk with about their spiritual life. I forget what they call it, but you said they said it was important."

"Forgot about that," confessed Leo sheepishly.

Later that afternoon, Leo called Pastor Jake. They arranged a time to talk, and a time to talk again, and a time to talk again. They have agreed to meet monthly for a while, at least a year. The principal focus of their conversation is Leo's spiritual walk.

God's free and unmerited gift of salvation in Jesus Christ embraces believers whether we feel it or not. The gift is ours, whether we feel it or not. At the same time, having a diminished sense of closeness with Christ or a waning sense of passion for one's ministry can challenge and distress a church worker. The ultimate danger is that one's heart, like Pharaoh's of old, can be hardened. This would be the greatest tragedy.

Faith's words reminded Leo that St. Andrew's had encouraged its staff to seek spiritual direction. As Leo explored this encouragement, he found a congregational policy that read: "All staff members are encouraged to have regular meetings with a spiritual advisor of their choosing, preferably a Christian spiritual advisor with a compatible theological and spiritual base. If there is a charge for such services, St. Andrew's will reimburse the worker at a rate of 90 percent to a maximum of $1,000 per year. The time taken for such meetings will be considered work time. Alternatively, our denominational health insurance coverage can be used to support work with a pastoral counselor from our managed care network. If the health insurance is used, St. Andrew's will support 90 percent of the cost of whatever co-pay is assessed."

St. Andrew's not only encouraged use of a spiritual advisor, it also facilitated and supported that use.

> Over time, Leo shared with Pastor Jake the details of his spiritual walk. Leo took advantage of the opportunity to share his specific sins, confess them, and receive Christ's absolution through Pastor Jake. Leo then began to participate in other spiritual growth opportunities St. Andrew's made available to its staff.

Remembering the Sabbath

The essential notion of celebrating the Sabbath or remembering the Sabbath is to cease work and to worship God, as Luther notes in his Explanation of the Third Commandment. How can a church worker, especially one who works on Sundays, honor the Sabbath? It is one thing to participate in voluntary activities on the Sabbath. It is quite another thing to work.

The routine of work and rest is set already in Genesis. Sabbath rest includes the worship of God. This is more, therefore, than a "day off." This is an intentional day. While it may be that the "whole day" concept needs to be flexibly applied, the intent of remembering the Sabbath— of having a significant period of time for rest and for worship—is part of the essential foundation of the life of the church worker. It is not in the best interests of staff, especially the pastors of the church, to think they are honoring the Sabbath-day imperative when they are leading worship.

St. Andrew's policy reads as follows: "Our staff needs time off to attend to their personal lives and to rest and worship God. Therefore, we expect a five-day workweek from our staff. From time to time, emergencies may arise that interfere with regularly scheduled time off. In those cases, we expect the worker to take compensatory time. Except in the most extreme and unusual circumstances, comp time should not be forfeited."

St. Andrew's encourages and facilitates the keeping of Sabbath. Their policy allows church workers to worship with family and to join Bible study and spiritual growth groups as participants, not leaders. Such a policy also allows workers to set limits on their availability. If pastor's day off is Friday, parishioners needing pastoral counseling need to schedule it on another day of the week.

SABBATICALS

Anecdotal reports suggest that after pastors have been in a church for four to seven years, many move on. If true, this suggests there may be a predictable process at work. At the four- or five- or six-year mark, workers may begin to question the "rightness" of being in a particular place. With that in mind, churches that want to support their workers might encourage them to set aside some time away for refreshment and study. This makes sense both for the renewal of the worker and for increased longevity at a particular place.

One could make the case that pastors who move after a short time in a given parish are trying to gain perspective and "begin again." A physical move may not be the best way to accomplish this. Rather than starting over in a new place, it might be healthier for the worker and better stewardship for the congregation if the pastor were simply to take some time away to refresh and renew. The term for this comes from the word for Sabbath—*sabbatical.*

Sabbaticals can be as brief as three months and as long as a year. They generally involve study and reflection on spiritual and ministry matters. Today sabbaticals are more traditionally associated with the academic community, but the idea has its roots in Leviticus 25. There, God mandated that His people allow the land to rest, to remain unplanted, every seven years. Even the earth must rest, recoup, and refresh!

St. Andrew's policy reads as follows: "After seven years of service, all ordained or commissioned staff are eligible for a sabbatical of six months. Planning for this sabbatical shall begin two years prior to its implementation. The worker shall submit a sabbatical plan to the Worker Support Team, which shall approve it. The plan will then be presented to the Leadership Council for approval. Sabbaticals are intended as a time of personal and professional renewal, study, and growth. Salary and benefits will continue throughout the sabbatical, though the worker is expected to apply for grants in support of the sabbatical. Any and all travel expenses are the responsibility of the staff member. Monthly summary reports of sabbatical activity are to be presented to the WST and, through this team, shared with the congregation as a whole. At the conclusion of the sabbatical, a summary report will be written, discussed with the WST, and presented to the congregation."

Church professionals have used sabbaticals for writing, study, travel, research, and more besides. In creating and adopting a policy, the congregation, institution, or school encourages and facilitates the taking of a sabbatical.

Shorter sabbaticals have also proven helpful. To encourage church workers to spend a day or two at a retreat center under the direction of a spiritual advisor can be very helpful. Retreats can be directed, that is, planned by the worker and a spiritual advisor who is available to the worker during the retreat. Retreats may also be undirected. Undirected retreats have no definitive agenda, but include a general plan such as, "I want to take a day to read the Scriptures, pray, and journal."

PRAYER TEAMS

> "One of the greatest things about being at St. Andrew's," reflected DCE Leo, "is that every week I receive a text message from a member of the WST, telling me which two members of St. Andrew's will be praying for me, my family, and my ministry that week. They ask about specific things for which I need prayer, and I reply. You have no idea how much that means to me and to Faith as well. Besides that," Leo continued, "every week in the services, the congregation prays for one specific staff member."

Many, many church workers would welcome prayer efforts like the one Leo describes. It is moving and encouraging knowing members of the congregation are praying for you. Even better than prayer in general is the opportunity to suggest specific prayer topics to a prayer team or prayer partner.

The prayer effort at St. Andrew's is organized and coordinated, not left to chance. Members pray for the workers' families, health, and ministry. They also pray that the workers' life and walk with Jesus will be rich and vital. In short, those who pray know about the particular vulnerabilities of the worker and address those vulnerabilities specifically.

SPEAKING PERSONALLY

As a church worker myself, I am responsible to be open and transparent about my personal vulnerabilities. However, I find it hard to take that risk, to open up my spiritual life, my struggles, my whole self to another human being, whether a spiritual director or a pastoral counselor.

It is even more difficult for workers whose congregation, school, or institution does not formally support such vulnerabilities. When it is expected and facilitated, encouraged and supported, that support makes a huge difference.

I teach an introductory course in pastoral counseling. In that course, I require that the students attend five personal counseling sessions or five sessions of spiritual direction. Students then write a summary of their work, and I take considerable time to respond to the summary. Students sometimes resist, but after a session or two, most find it valuable. I think this is a good sign.

My students, like the church workers they will one day become, face spiritual dangers because of their studies and their chosen vocation. I see it as part of my responsibility to understand that danger and work intentionally to address it.

CHAPTER FIFTEEN

COMPENSATION

Few church workers enter their vocation hoping to become rich. Like those who choose other service-oriented vocations, most church workers are motivated by the rewards of caring for others. They place less emphasis on making money for themselves. This service motivation, when combined with a congregation's expectation that their workers live selfless, sacrificial lives, often creates an environment in which it's hard to have basic conversations about compensation.

Church workers who advocate for a larger salary or better benefits open themselves up to criticism for being self-serving rather than Christ-serving. On the other hand, church workers who live with ongoing financial strain or perch on the edge of financial ruin need a forum in which to effectively discuss and negotiate this. Otherwise, they will likely live with the effects of suppressed, unhappy, anxious, and even angry feelings. Dissatisfaction about inadequate compensation makes workers targets for "the flaming darts of the evil one" (Ephesians 6:16).

That significant compensation concerns drain energy from church workers should not come as a surprise. In 1943, pioneer psychologist Abraham Maslow published his now-famous hierarchy of needs. His basic premise is that fundamental human needs must be met (adequately, not perfectly) before a person can move into creative, growth producing behaviors.

Maslow found that a person's need for oxygen, food, and other biological necessities form the foundation. Second come security needs. Adequate compensation fits in this category. The needs in these foundational categories must be met before people can function at their best, their most creative. Among other things, this is why compensation matters so much. Lack of adequate compensation drains energy and creativity.

Additional research has shown that while increased compensation has little long-term positive effect, the perception of under-compensation has significant long-term negative effect. Thus, we might think of compensation as a foundation on which to build; it is not the building itself.

Most church workers don't strive to be wealthy. Instead, compensation is only a means to a greater end, that is, being able to carry out their vocation creatively and well. In one study of parochial school teachers, researchers found that the most important factors in vocational satisfaction were:

1. A positive relationship with the principal.

2. Positive relationships with other faculty members.

3. Positive relationships with students' parents.

4. The ability to be good teachers for their pupils.

Compensation contributed to satisfaction, but it fell further down on the list.

In contrast, though, when the teachers were asked to

name the greatest threats to their continuing to teach in the church, under-compensation topped the list. They weren't sure they could continue to teach because of insufficient pay.

> Ascension Church, with a membership of 215 adults, is nestled in a town of 17,000. It is served by one pastor and one full-time administrative assistant. The congregation participates actively in the community, particularly in support of the local food pantry and the regional social service agency. It thinks of itself as a friendly, vibrant congregation, and it has held its own in its smaller-town environment by developing a robust, welcoming style and assertive evangelism programs.

> Pastor John has served Ascension for seven years. He was granted a six-month sabbatical in his sixth year and used the time to study and to visit growing smaller-town churches like Ascension, not limiting his study to churches of his own denomination. He also spent a week of his sabbatical at a retreat center under the guidance of a spiritual director. He returned from the sabbatical experience energized and renewed.

> Ascension formed a Worker Support Team several years ago. Its members had asked Pastor John to include compensation packages in his sabbatical study of congregations like Ascension. He forwarded his findings to Joyce, a member of the WST. Joyce then wrote a summary report. She included Pastor's findings, salary guidelines provided by the regional judicatory of Ascen-

sion's denomination, and compensation information from churches in towns nearby.

Joyce's report confirmed what some members of the WST had feared: Pastor John's compensation was somewhat less, though not substantially less, than compensation packages of other parishes like Ascension, though many of those parishes did not offer a sabbatical.

"Pastor John is an outstanding pastor," Joyce wrote in her report, "and we need to put together a compensation package that is above the average."

Later in the report Joyce wrote, "We will need to talk with Pastor John directly about his compensation, as well as about how we view the quality of his pastorate here. But these are two different concerns: comparable compensation and our evaluation of his performance. Our compensation package should be fair and of high quality regardless of who occupies the pastoral office."

After Joyce submitted her report, the WST went to work. They knew their church's health insurance plan had a number of different coverage options, each option with a different price tag. The lower the coverage and higher the deductible, the lower the premium.

Joyce's report showed that many similar local churches had resisted the impulse to save money by buying less health insurance coverage. Even the ones that opted for less-expensive, high-deductible options put monies into a separate account to help make up for their workers' out-of-pocket costs. Ascension's WST recommended that next year's budget include more comprehensive health care insurance coverage for their pastor.

When the WST moved on to consider salary, they found that their pastor earned about 5 percent less than the median (average) salary paid to pastors in area congregations like Ascension. They resolved to propose a 9 percent salary increase to the Finance Committee when the budget was being created. This represented a 7 percent pay increase to bring Pastor John's salary above the median and a 2 percent increase that was consistent with cost-of-living inflation. Everyone knew this would stretch the budget. But, as Joyce wrote, "We want to be a congregation that treats its staff well, because that is just who we are. We also want our staff to have an excellent compensation package so that, freed from a lot of the anxiety concerning their capacity to make ends meet, they are able to use their energy in the service of Ascension."

Finally, Joyce wrote: "This process of looking at congregations like Ascension has really been eye-opening for Pastor John and for me. I recommend we conduct a similar study for the position of administrative assistant."

Consider what Ascension's WST did here:

- They already had a Worker Support Team in place.

Team members were energized and focused on worker issues, concerns, and needs.

- They advocated for their pastor's best interests in compensation conversations so he didn't have to. They became his voice.

- The team looked at "compensation" as a package; they didn't focus solely on salary. They understood that one area affects others. They knew that subscribing to a health insurance plan with a higher deductible represents a decrease in available income for the worker and his family, and is therefore a salary decrease.

- Members of the team kept in mind a vision or a picture of the kind of congregation they were and wanted to be. For example, they didn't want to be "average," and therefore their compensation would not be "average" either—within budgetary constraints.

- The WST did its homework. They researched comparable situations. They used the resources their denomination provided. They collected and analyzed as much data as they could.

- They did not just report on their research. They made specific, actionable recommendations.

- They separated their study of compensation from the process of performance evaluation. They wanted create the best possible compensation package, given the budget and the results of their research.

- They expanded the research process to include staff positions in addition to that of the pastor. This will help to avoid jealousy and competition between people working together on the same staff.

In addition to salary, other benefits factor into a church worker's total compensation. We will now consider a few of the most common.

HEALTH INSURANCE

The general trend in many organizations related to health insurance coverage is (1) to cover only the "employee," (2) to share the cost of the coverage with the "employee," and (3) to search out coverage that is as inexpensive as possible.

None of these trends are fully supportive of paid staff. All negatively affect total compensation. When churches adopt any of these approaches, a corresponding increase in salary to cover the loss of spendable income should take place. For instance, if a congregation decides to cover only the worker's health insurance, dropping coverage for the family because family coverage would cost the congregation an additional $700 per month, then consideration should be given to increasing the salary of the church worker by that amount.

It is almost always possible to find cheaper health insurance, especially if those covered are younger and healthier. Most denominational health insurance plans cover the whole spectrum of church workers, both younger and older, those with current medication conditions and those with none identified. These plans should be supported simply because they effectively cover all workers. The point of health insurance coverage is for those who are currently healthy to support others who are ill. Over time, everyone in the plan benefits from the help of others.

It is almost always possible to find cheaper health insurance, too, if the cheaper policy covers much less and has higher deductibles. Even some denominational health insurance plans offer various options. Higher deductibles mean lower costs. Supportive congregations that switch to these plans will use a substantial portion of the savings to offset the increased deductible costs workers must pay.

Churches need to balance the competing needs of cost savings and worker support. If the balance tips, it should tip on the side of worker support. Any shift toward less coverage or higher deductibles represents a loss of income to the worker. That, in turn, undermines the foundation on which worker creativity and energy is built. Most times, church workers will not or cannot advocate for themselves. Other voices need to speak up.

HOUSING PROVIDED

Some congregations offer housing in the form of a parsonage or teacherage. This is a congregation-owned home in which the worker lives, rent-free. Often, the cash salary the worker receives is less than if a worker were to seek his or her own housing, sometimes substantially less.

Two concerns often arise in connection with this process: (1) workers do not have an opportunity to build up equity in the way they might if they owned their own home, and (2) living on congregational property can create questions related to boundaries, access, and upkeep.

The equity issue can easily be solved by the creation of an equity fund on behalf of the church worker. The congregation maintains this restricted fund for use by the worker if he or she purchases a house while serving the congregation. If the worker moves, money in the fund is given to the worker for use as a down payment in a new location. As an alternative, the worker's cash salary could be increased with the understanding that the worker will place the designated amount into a housing fund for future use.

Admittedly, Finance Committees may struggle with this recommendation. However, it is important; if a worker moves to a different church, one with no parsonage, finding money for a down payment on a home is likely to be difficult. The creation of an equity fund helps solve this problem. Some denominations require churches with a parsonage to create an equity fund.

RETIREMENT PLANS

Many church workers pay 100 percent of their own Social Security tax. As of this writing, it is a flat 15 percent assessed on the entire cash salary of the church worker, including any housing allowance the congregation grants. In most other jobs, the employer would be responsible for half of this tax, but because the tax laws categorize many church workers as "self-employed," they are required to pay it all. Given this, it is not unreasonable that a congregation would offer a payment to the worker designed to offset half of this tax.

Additionally, many denominations have their own retirement plans into which congregations contribute. Full participation on behalf of the worker is necessary and vital.

Sometimes churches make available to their workers tax-sheltered retirement plans that include the possibility of an employer match. For instance, when workers contribute 3 percent of their salary to the tax-sheltered retirement plan, the congregation matches this at the rate of 50 cents on the dollar, contributing 1.5 percent of the base salary.

Because it connects to such basic security needs, and because it is often, perhaps erroneously, seen as a statement about worth and value, a discussion about compensation is almost always somewhat tense. The better discussions occur in an atmosphere of trust and safety where relationships have been formed that are healthy and meaningful conversations have already taken place.

A FEW CONCLUDING THOUGHTS

It is much harder to talk about compensation if that conversation comes as the first serious dialogue the church worker has had with congregational leadership. Thus, as I have said throughout this book, it is essential that church workers and leaders work actively and intentionally to build positive relationships with one another before serious matters arise. When relationships are frayed, it is hard to talk about money. In such circumstances, casual comments can easily convey unspoken messages of unhappiness and discontent—from the worker to church leadership and from church leadership to the worker. Money should never be used as a weapon in such a conversation.

Having a compensation policy in place, as did St. Andrew's, means that a church has already engaged their workers in significant conversations. In that case, annual or semi-annual discussions about compensation simply continue along the lines of that tradition.

Decisions about compensation should not follow in lockstep with the congregation's budgetary problems or joys. It is not healthy to conclude, "We are having trouble making our budget so let's cut staff salary by 8 percent." A more healthy direction would sound like this: "We are having trouble making our budget, so let's examine our giving patterns, reflect on our stewardship, and see where cuts, if necessary, need to be made. And let's involve the members of our staff in this process too."

SPEAKING PERSONALLY

Over the years I have received numerous communications from church workers (or their spouses or children) telling some very painful stories about how churches use money to send a message of displeasure. Some churches have even decided to make a situation so financially uncomfortable that the worker had no choice but to seek another position. I have been surprised and at times shocked at these things: (1) how money is sometimes used as a weapon and (2) how difficult it sometimes is for church workers, including myself, to talk directly about this, and, correspondingly (3) how indirectly congregational leadership may deal with this.

When church leaders adopt an approach, either of indirect conversation or of using money to get at other concerns, they almost never engage the worker in an ongoing conversation about why they are dissatisfied, nor do they help develop a plan to remediate the problem(s). These things should not happen in the Body of Christ.

I admit that at times I have trouble dealing with conflict. It's also hard for me to talk about money. My natural inclination is to avoid all such conversations. This is not how I should be as a member of the Body of Christ, nor should this be for other church workers.

Congregations should not ignore conflict. They should speak forthrightly about money. But we all need safe spaces and secure relationships if we are to talk about difficult things. It is my job to do my part to develop such spaces for people who work with and for me. It is the task of congregations to develop such spaces for their workers so that honest, forthright, and caring discussions about compensation can take place.

CHAPTER SIXTEEN

TIME AND WORKLOAD

Carla pulled Joyce aside. Joyce served as the director of Christian outreach (DCO) at Bethlehem Church. "Got a couple of minutes to talk?" Carla asked.

"Sure," replied Joyce. The two walked together toward a small room away from the church office. "What's this about?" Joyce wondered.

For several weeks, Carla had been thinking about how to start this conversation. Joyce was doing great work at Bethlehem. In her position for only three years, she had mobilized small groups in the congregation. The groups had considered strategies for outreach in their community of around 25,000 people. Then, they had begun to implement the strategy they developed. "Joyce really lives up to her title," Carla thought. Carla respected Joyce for her work, and she also counted her a friend.

"Joyce," began Carla, "A lot of people think you are doing a great job here at Bethlehem, and I hope you know I am one of those people. I want to thank you for it. You've helped us make some good changes, and Bethlehem has started to thrive, thanks to them."

"Thanks," replied Joyce, "I am thankful that the Spirit has been so open with such blessings."

"I have a concern, though," continued Carla.

"Oh," mumbled Joyce with a trace of anxiety in her voice. "Here we go," she thought, "There's always a negative to go with every positive."

Raised in a hard-working, success-oriented family, Joyce was used to faint praise for a job well done, followed by messages like, "It could have been done better," or "Don't get a swelled head." Those messages from her family of origin meant she never felt truly satisfied with her performance, even now as a middle-aged adult. Even when things went well, there was more and more to do. Joyce had never truly learned to enjoy the satisfaction of a job well done.

Granted, things were going very well in a position she really loved! Granted, her relationships with other staff members seemed excellent! "So what am I doing wrong?" Joyce asked herself.

Carla continued, "My concern is that your job is taking up too much of your life. You are very good at what you do. But you're doing more and more of it as things at Bethlehem move forward. Your plate looks pretty full to me. I don't know how you can squeeze one more thing on it. But still, you rise to every occasion. You do it in wonderful ways. That's one thing I really like and respect in you. But we all have limits! I'm concerned that you may be reaching the limits of what you can do and still stay healthy. What do you think?"

"I think you've got a good point," Joyce responded. Inside she felt relieved. At least Carla didn't sound critical, nor was she issuing a call to do more. She just seemed genuinely concerned.

Besides, Carla was pretty much on-target. Joyce was seeing less of her teenage children. And her relationship with her husband, Bert, while strong, had lost some of the closeness they had once enjoyed.

"There is a lot going on," Joyce said, "and there is a lot to be done. Sometimes I think I am on a merry-go-round and other times I feel like a ping-pong ball being bounced from task to task," she admitted as her voice faltered.

Clearly, Carla's words had touched a nerve that needed to be explored. Joyce began to hope this might be an opportunity to consider what was happening and, perhaps, to plan a way to tackle the issues head on.

Already in a strong relationship with Joyce, Carla used her friendship to raise an important concern. In another context, if Carla had been a member of the church's Worker Support Team (WST), for example, she might have placed workload discussions on that team's agenda or suggested they address it as part of an annual, larger conversation.

What happens now? What can Carla (and Joyce) do

to remove the "perhaps" from the plan to "tackle things head-on"? Here are some ideas:

- Staff members might work together to discuss time and workload management. Perhaps an outside consultant could facilitate the conversation. Congregational leaders will need to be involved at some point in this discussion. If the church has a WST, its members would make ideal participants.

- Staff members could begin by studying their current use of time. Each person could keep a time log for two to four weeks. This will give everyone a baseline from which to work. Summary charts will be useful as, based on the time logs, they help visualize reality. Notes as simple as "Our staff sleeps on average 42 hours per week, 6 hours per night," signals a possible concern. A note like this might raise a red flag too: "On average, staff spend only 1½ hours per day with their family." Specific comments, coupled with charts and graphs, can move discussion from general impressions to specific realities.

- Members of the WST might research time at work expectations along with the compensation research suggested in the previous chapter. How many hours do other, comparable congregations, schools, or church institutions expect? How do these organizations establish policies for workload, days off, vacations, and the like? A regional judicatory staff might be able to offer some helpful information as well.

- Congregational leaders could work with staff to

develop priorities. What is most important? To what requests could and should a staff member say no? How will congregational leaders support that response? In the community of faith, no church worker should be making a unilateral decision about his or her use of time. Such decisions should be mutual and based on the strategic priorities of both the congregation and the worker.

■ The WST or another appropriate group of congregational leaders should write job descriptions for all workers. These documents need to include both boundaries and priorities. If, for instance, the church has prioritized member contact and community outreach, then the church staff will likely spend fewer hours in the office and more time out and about in the community. If a congregation wants its workers to have personal time and time with family, members will refrain from phoning on the worker's day off, except in emergencies, and workers should be expected to take compensatory time off to make up for personal time off lost to legitimate emergencies.

■ Congregations should establish reasonable time-at-work expectations. Many time management resources divide the week into twenty-one segments: morning, afternoon, and evening over a seven-day period. During how many of those segments should a staff member be working? Ten? That would constitute roughly a 40-hour week. Fifteen? That is morning, afternoon, and evening five days a week. Again, such planning should not be done unilaterally by the church worker. Without the support of congregational leadership, the worker faces an uphill time management battle.

- Churches also need to establish, publicize, and honor staff vacation days. How many vacation days should congregations grant? Two weeks? Four weeks? Six weeks? Certainly two weeks is an absolute minimum. Again, members of the WST or other members of the congregation with a similar charge should research the policies of other congregations, schools, and church institutions. Again, the regional judicatory leadership may be a source of helpful information.

- Congregations need to consider granting sabbaticals as discussed in previous chapters.

- Churches need to establish continuing education policies. Workers should not be expected to use their vacation time or their own financial resources in support of continuing education. Some denominations require continuing education for their clergy. Almost all teachers have continuing education requirements. Workers who are growing professionally and intellectually are the kind of workers congregations, schools, and church institutions want.

Because church workers are, in general, focused on service and on other people, they are sometimes reluctant to take their days off or use their vacation days. While no worker wants church leaders to micromanage their days off or vacation days, leaders can support, encourage, and sometimes prod staff to take time away. For a number of different personal reasons, many church workers have a tendency to believe that they let people down when they take time off. They have difficulty seeing or believing that time off is regenerative for them and actually helps them be more productive and useful when they return. Accountability around issues of time off is an important support function for the congregational leadership.

> "I can't believe it!" shouted Louis, a long-time member with a reputation for being a bit of a curmudgeon. Associate Pastor Jim was walking to the parking lot with Louis, each headed to his own car.
>
> "Can't believe what?" responded Pastor Jim, knowing he would probably regret asking.
>
> "I hear the elders are checking up on you, making sure you're taking all your days off and all your vacation time. What's the deal? Aren't y'all big enough to take care of yourselves?"
>
> Pastor Jim sighed. A couple of thoughts passed through his head. One was that he was not responsible for the development of this account-ability and support process. It was the initiative of the WST. Another was that he really liked the support. He could take time off without feeling guilty—at least, not very guilty. Besides, the congregation had an established grievance pro-cedure. If Louis had an issue, he knew he should be going to the correct people—in this case, the WST.

"Louis," Pastor Jim began, "You seem to have a concern, and maybe even some feelings of distress. Since we have a process for raising concerns in this congregation, I think you should take it up with Alma. She is the chairperson of the WST. She can then plan with you how to communicate your concern. I'll give Alma a call myself to let her know you'll be contacting her. As you know, we have a covenant with each other to do that."

"I don't want to talk to Alma," Louis said reactively.

"Well," replied the pastor, "We have all agreed on what to do when we have concerns and disagreements. I'd encourage you to talk with her as you agreed to do when we set up the covenant. Meanwhile, I'll let Alma know that you have this concern."

"Oh, all right," said Louis.

"One more thing," continued Pastor Jim. "I like this. The support and accountability it provides is helpful to me and, I pray, helps me be a better pastor."

In this case, Pastor Jim referenced the congregational covenant and grievance procedures, and did not engage Louis in a dispute about a policy that is the responsibility of someone else. He reflected Louis' concerns, but did not join in conversation around them. He stood his ground, based on the agreements and promises all members had made about how to handle grievances and conflict.

> Louis did approach Alma. "I have a gripe . . ." he began as he explained his objections.

> "Thanks for raising your concerns," Alma replied. "I'd like to talk a little bit about what our thinking was on the WST when we set the workload policy for staff in place. And if our talk doesn't get at your concerns in a satisfactory way, then the next step is for you and others who have similar concerns to come to our next team meeting so that we can talk directly about this."

Alma steered Louis' concerns in a productive direction. She would listen to his opinions and respond to them. If he still didn't agree, he had another forum in which to air his thoughts. In the process, Louis may not change his views, but those views will have been heard and his objections will have been taken seriously.

When we encourage church workers to take time off and to advocate for a reasonable policy concerning vacation time and compensatory time, we put them in an awkward position. Self-advocacy can easily be misunderstood as self-promotion or even selfishness. But without appropriate benefits, including time off, the work and its stress will drain staff energy and enthusiasm. It will also provide a fertile field for the "schemes of the devil" (Ephesians 6:11). Church workers need someone to speak up for them, to consider their needs and the needs of the congregation, and to create workable policies. It's just one more reason congregations need to put in place a Worker Support Team.

A final note of caution: Policies focused on workload, vacation, continuing education, and sabbaticals should never be used as vehicles to express a congregation's dissatisfaction with the performance or personal style of a church worker. Nor should conversations around workload happen before a strong working relationship between the worker and lay leaders is in place. First comes the building of positive relationships; then comes the discussion of personnel issues.

SPEAKING PERSONALLY

For twenty years, I have written a monthly column, "Pressure Points" in the *Reporter*, the official newspaper of the LCMS. The column has focused on difficult questions churches and their workers face. Some of the most painful of these questions have concerned compensation and the church worker's use of time.

The pain usually comes because the congregation in question has hurled general accusations about how the worker is prioritizing time and effort, while no one in leadership has specified the congregation's priorities. Distrust quickly grows on both sides in circumstances like that. Then, it erupts into generic, global conflict. In such a context, solutions are difficult to find.

Let me give an example. Pastor Smith's church expected him to visit and care for the elderly and shut-ins. Instead of saying that or saying it in a way Pastor Smith heard it, the leaders asked instead that the pastor produce daily logs outlining his use of time. On the surface, the conflict seemed to roil over time management issues in general, when, at its core, the conflict actually concerned the pastor's failure to focus on a specific activity the congregation held as a major (though unspoken) priority. More direct discussion about priorities and expectations would have helped. So would a job description in which specific expectations were outlined.

Sometimes the time management questions I answered in the column revolved around a pastor's use of the Internet. Most times, congregational leaders had attempted to address their dissatisfaction indirectly, as in the example above, asking for time logs or similar evidence of how the pastor was spending his time. Often, the leaders insisted that the pastor take a time management workshop.

Time management was not the real issue. The leaders and pastor needed to engage in direct discussion about the expectations the church had for their pastor. Here, too, everyone would have benefited from a specific job description that would have identified these expectations. Then the congregation's leaders could have evaluated their pastor on the basis of whether or not the outcomes from the job description were being met.

But even the creation of a job description does not well serve church workers or the congregation until strong working relationships and alliances have been forged or repaired. Failures in relationship cannot be fixed by focusing on issues of compensation, use of time, or the creation of job descriptions.

CHAPTER SEVENTEEN

MARRIAGE AND FAMILY

"What a two weeks this had been!" mused Mary, wife of newly-installed Pastor Charles. "Come to think of it, the last two or three months have been a blur. Packing up, coming to Resurrection, unpacking, getting settled, figuring things out, wondering how I will fit in, concern about Charles and whether his new position will make his time even more rare for our young children. And me! Worrying. Flurrying. Saying good-bye. Saying hello. Crying. Laughing. Mourning. Rejoicing. Good grief, what a tapestry of feelings. And all the stuff I still need to get done!

"I don't know what I would have done without Susan and Gail. They have been just terrific. As soon as Charles received his call, they phoned me. Even before he accepted the call, they offered to answer my questions about Resurrection, the community, and the surrounding area. They called themselves liaisons on behalf of something called the Worker Support Team.

"I did have some questions about schools and possible opportunities for me to work, at least part-time, as a preschool teacher. They sent me Web sites from local school districts and a list of all the preschools in the community, including the one at Resurrection. Wow!

"When Charles told Resurrection he had accepted their call, they phoned back to say how pleased they were. They also repeated their offer to answer questions and concerns. And they put us in touch with a couple of real estate agents— not members of the church, but highly recommended.

"On the day of the move, Susan and Gail brought in cold drinks and food for lunch. Then other people brought dinner that night. Gail even thought to bring a packet full of information about the town. This was not just the printed stuff from the Chamber of Commerce, as good as that was. There was also a map showing the locations of supermarkets and drug stores. There was a listing of some medical doctors, including pediatricians for our kids. There were applications for library cards, additional information about schools, preschools, and child care—and a list of several mature Resurrection youth who could babysit.

"Susan and Gail also brought several young adults from Resurrection who offered to move boxes around for us or to go to the store to get us things. It is really hard to describe the sense of hospitality that Charles and I felt. Even our children felt it. Moving is hard. I left many good friends. I mourn the loss of day-to-day contact with them. But I am hopeful. These folks really seem to get this hospitality thing.

"One of the best things was that no one mentioned Resurrection on moving day—issues and concerns, I mean. Really, no one tried to get an oar in the water. Instead, they all talked about the community, its resources, and what we needed to know to get settled in. They just seemed to care about how we were doing.

"Then, at Charles' installation, Gail and Susan made sure to introduce me to anyone within range. No one can predict the future, but I'm pretty optimistic! Susan and Gail describe their function, at least at the beginning, as one of support and translation. They want to be helpful and they want me to look to them should I have questions about the culture, activities, or ways-of-doing-things of Resurrection and in the community. That's the translation part. They offered to help me in the transition into this new place. These are two very warm and caring people. But it is also clear that they are sanctioned by Resurrection. The church has intentionally put them in place as volunteers to serve their new pastor and his family in this way. It's remarkable!"

Resurrection clearly cares about their pastor's relationships with his wife and children. It demonstrates this by intentionally assigning people to meet the needs of his wife and family. The story of Mary (above) illustrates warm, welcoming hospitality during the new pastor's transition and arrival at Resurrection. Of course, it's vital that the support continue beyond the first phase of Pastor Charles's ministry.

Much of the research that deals with stress in the workplace discusses the multiplying effect that marital and family stressors can have. Rather than adding to workplace stress, family stress seems to multiply it! On the other hand, stable marriage and family relationships can serve as buffers against job burnout and workplace stress. Thus, healthy congregations pay attention to family units, as well as to individual workers. Care for staff includes care for the marriages and families of workers. It is a great investment in the well-being of both the church and its workers.

The story that began this chapter gave many examples of supportive behaviors during the first few days of their new pastor's tenure. How can congregations provide ongoing support to the families of their workers? Here are some ideas.

Spouse

☐ Applaud, foster, and accept spousal differences. Not all spouses of church workers will fit the stereotypical mold, nor will they want the same level of involvement in the congregation. Don't make one spouse the yardstick by which you measure all others. Some spouses will plunge into church and school activities with both feet; others will want limited involvement. Some spouses will themselves have professional careers; some will want to volunteer or focus on their children instead. Some spouses will be outgoing; others will be more shy and reserved. Some will want to influence the direction of the congregation or school; others will stay apart from such influence.

Healthy congregations encourage spouses to make the decisions that best fit their family and personal situation.

☐ Expand the role and function of the Worker Support Team to include the spouses of workers. Appoint a member or two who will have this as their primary agenda. These liaisons can partner with the spouse in terms of emotional support, practical help, and translating community culture. (See the comments about "Who Helps Me See What Is?" in Chapter 12.)

☐ Provide health care coverage for the spouse. Family coverage is losing favor among businesses, primarily because it is costly. However, covering the worker's spouse clearly communicates the commitment of the congregation, school, or institution to the health and well-being of the worker. Not providing such coverage can create serious financial challenges and communicate a failure to care.

☐ Offer support for the spouse's personal spiritual growth. Almost everything discussed concerning the Wholeness Wheel (Chapter 10) also applies to each worker's spouse. Some have observed that the most under-pastored person in the Christian community is the pastor's wife. Most congregants see the pastor of the church as his wife's pastor too. But how can one person actually fill both roles? Attention must be given to the spiritual needs of pastors' wives. This is true across church vocations. Is the spouse of an associate pastor going to seek pastoral care from the senior pastor who is also the "boss" of the associate, so to speak? How about the spouse of a church school-teacher? Or the spouse of a DCE? Relationships on church staffs are quite complex. Pastoral care, at its best, needs to be free of that complexity.

☐ Pray for spouses by name, just as you pray for members of the church staff themselves. Create prayer partners who will commit to this. Let the spouses know who is praying for them and when.

MARRIAGE

☐ Accept and cultivate differences in marital relation-ships. Not all marriages look the same. Some couples often hold hands and are outwardly affectionate; others appear more distant in public. Some seem perfectly matched; others seem quite the opposite of each other. Not all church worker marriages fit a stereotypical mold. If the worker's marital style differs significantly from the culture of the church and the larger community, use the WST to discuss this with the worker and her/his spouse, but only after a posi-tive relationship has already been established.

☐ Offer time and at least some financial support to make it possible for couples to attend marriage enrichment events or some other retreat designed to keep the cou-ple's relationship fresh and vital.

☐ Create healthy workplace practices, provide ade-quate compensation, and give appropriate time off to workers so they can attend to the marital relationship God has given them. Do not allow the worker's commitments at church to turn into a "vocational affair" in which the church's expectations displace the high vocation of wife or husband.

☐ Place questions such as, "How is your work and workload here affecting your marriage?" into the ongoing conversation congregational leaders have with individual church staff. Preferably, this kind of discussion would happen in the safety of the WST.

☐ Encourage couples to worship together whenever possible. This could include worshiping together at a different church when another parish's worship schedule accommodates it.

☐ Be sure your health insurance plan includes marital counseling as a benefit. Many denominational health insurance plans include this, at least at the employee assistance plan (EAP) level.

☐ Lift up all staff marriages by name in the congregation's worship services at least once each year.

☐ Develop and support creative options to strengthen marriages of staff. This is one place where Satan can find a foothold and, sometimes, bring down an entire ministry. Proactively confront and deflect this attack!

CHILDREN

☐ Accept the fact that staff members' children will come with many different styles, temperaments, abilities, and interests. Not all children of church workers look alike, nor will they all want the same level of involvement in the congregation. Do not expect them to fit into some ideal mold. Do not use the behavior of previous workers' children as the yardstick by which all future children are judged.

☐ Encourage the WST to include staff children under their umbrella of concern. Appoint a liaison person(s) whose primary focus is the care and support of the worker's child.

☐ Provide health care coverage for the family.

☐ Offer healthy workplace practices, adequate compensation, and appropriate time off for staff so they can attend to family relationships. No worker's job should turn into an ersatz family that displaces the high vocation of parent.

☐ Offer support for the children's spiritual growth. If pastors' wives are under-pastored, so are their children.

☐ Pray by name for the children of all church workers in the congregation. Develop prayer partners who will commit to doing this. Let the children know who is praying for them and when.

All this takes energy and planning. But Satan has invested energy and developed a plan to undermine the efforts of church leaders. You can be sure that plan includes the families of church workers (see Chapter 1). Our Lord has told us how to counter Satan's schemes:

Speaking the truth in love, we are to grow up in every way into Him who is the head, into Christ, from whom the whole body, joined and held together by every joint with which it is equipped, when each part is working properly, makes the body grow so that it builds itself up in love. (Ephesians 4:15–16)

> ## SATAN HAS INVESTED ENERGY AND DEVELOPED A PLAN TO UNDERMINE THE EFFORTS OF CHURCH LEADERS.

Speaking Personally

I cannot count the spouses and children of church workers I have counseled over the years. Many of their stories are painful and heart wrenching. I will never name them publicly, of course, but this chapter is most certainly dedicated to them.

Without their stories, I could not have written this chapter. My hope is that because I've heard their stories, this chapter has more credibility, depth, and helpfulness.

For every, "The son of a pastor shouldn't behave that way," church members should provide ten "Jesus forgives you all your sins and loves you with an everlasting love."

For every, "The daughter of a teacher should be more studious in her work," church leaders should provide ten "Jesus loves and cares for you and is with you as you work to find your way through school and your path through life."

For every, "Just look happy and holy today," church leaders should initiate ten conversations about what is actually happening in a person's life, even if that person is the spouse or child of a church worker.

For every criticism, there should be a hundred prayers of support, beseeching the throne of God on behalf of the spouse or child of the church worker.

Praise God, not all the stories I hear are negative. There are wonderful stories of welcoming and hospitable congregations who intentionally foster the health and well-being, not only of the church worker but also of his/ her spouse and their children. My prayer is that the readers of this book take the lead in helping to write more of these wonderful stories.

When Things Go Downhill

Things do not always go well between church workers and the congregations, schools, and institutions they serve. Things do not always go well in the lives of the church workers themselves. Difficulties emerge and fissures open. Even so, God calls congregations and their workers to deal with negative events and circumstances in as constructive and healthy a way as possible.

We lay aside the vision of perfect harmony and flawless relationships, knowing these are not possible in our fallen, sinful world. Workers cannot expect to serve perfect people in perfect settings. Likewise, churches understand that their workers will struggle with life's temptations and personal shortcomings. We are all "poor, miserable sinners," as our liturgy reminds us. We commit, instead, to a vision of mutual care, forgiveness, and support.

When church workers stumble, it is not helpful to ignore it. The best support a congregation, school, or institution of the church can provide under these circumstances is to engage the worker directly, to have frank conversations, and then work together toward positive solutions. The sooner the better—before small problems grow into large ones.

The chapters in this section will explore a few of the

things that can take the relationship between workers and those they serve downhill, behaviors that are unhealthy and destructive. These chapters will also explore issues such as personality disorders, affective (feeling) disorders, and addictive disorders.

This section is, obviously, darker than the rest of the book. Yet it is necessary that those who want to support church workers have at least a cursory understanding of the more troublesome issues and concerns that may arise. That way, potentially toxic problems can be met early on with a constructive response.

CHAPTER EIGHTEEN

FRACTURED RELATIONSHIPS

It takes two to tango and five to line dance.

When relationships fracture, the interpersonal space between people becomes unsafe. Accusations and blame replace expressions of comfort and care. Defensive maneuvers replace transparency and vulnerability. Even in the church, people say to one another, "It's your fault," instead of "How can we work on this together?"

The process of projection and blame goes way back, back to Eden and our first parents. When God confronted Adam and Eve with their sin, Adam said, "The woman whom you gave to be with me, she gave me fruit of the tree, and I ate" (Genesis 3:12). When God questioned Eve, she responded, "The serpent deceived me, and I ate" (Genesis 3:13). Neither assumed personal responsibility. Note this key dynamic!

The text reveals no evidence that Adam said, "Yes, God, I ate and I repent. I beg You, please forgive me." There is no evidence that Eve said, "Yes, God, I took the fruit, I tempted Adam to eat, and I ate myself. I am truly sorry. Forgive me." Absent was the capacity, or at least the willingness, to look inside themselves, to take responsibility for their own behavior, and to confess their disobedience to God in true repentance.

Certainly, Adam and Eve felt afraid and vulnerable.

Adam revealed this when he told God, "I heard the sound of You in the garden, and I was afraid, because I was naked, and I hid myself" (Genesis 3:10).

It was not easy for our first parents, nor is it easy even for God's people today, to step forward interpersonally naked, vulnerable, to take responsibility. From a sinner's point of view, it is much safer to blame someone else.

> The meeting between Pastor Ed and the Board of Elders had become tense as the evening wore on. Noah, the chair of the elders, was at his wits' end. "You haven't been making the number of calls we told you to make," Noah lashed out. "We've been over this again and again, but still you are not doing what you are supposed to do!"

> Stung, Pastor Ed responded: "And you are not showing respect for the pastoral office. I determine what is necessary for the spiritual care of my people, not you. You are not trained to do this. You are not called by God to the pastoral office!"

> "That's arrogant and self-centered. I expect better from a pastor," Noah scoffed. Several positive headshakes around the table confirmed Noah's opinion. Jamie didn't nod. He was the newest member of the Elder Board, elected less than a year ago. He sat frozen, not at all sure what he could or should do. He knew that everyone had agreed on the importance of evangelism and shut-in calls. Even Pastor Ed had agreed. So Jamie was puzzled that Pastor Ed had not followed through.

"I wonder what is really going on with him?" Jamie thought to himself. But more angry words interrupted his musings.

"We pay your salary. You're supposed to do what you're told to do. You're supposed to be sensitive to the needs of others. For crying out loud, didn't they teach you at the seminary to put the needs of others before your own?"

"I am sensitive to the needs of others," insisted Pastor Ed. "But I'm not going to be controlled like I'm a puppet of some kind." He wanted to leave, but he could not. So, he sat steaming. There was no way could he bring forward his best ideas when the discussion later turned to other matters.

Noah, on the other hand, concluded on the spot he would not run for reelection to the Elder Board. He continued to chair the meeting, but with little enthusiasm and energy.

When they finally adjourned the meeting, everyone breathed a sigh of relief. The closing prayer, benediction, and "good-nights" were frosty, at best.

Most of the energy in this conversation was negative, and it was directed toward other people in the room. The group directed very little energy toward solving the problem of ways to provide the best possible spiritual care for those who needed it. Worse still, this situation is almost certain to deteriorate into a win-lose conflict or even an impassioned, "I'm going to get you before you get me" battle. Such impasses often end with the pastor leaving and one or more elders resigning. The wounds of this conflict will stay with everyone for a long, long time. Clearly, this conflict did not begin in this meeting. There is certainly a history behind it.

How can these relationships be made whole? How can the processes we learned from our first parents be replaced with more holy, health-giving ones? There are two possible alternatives. Neither is necessarily better than the other. I present them here as options.

The first involves Jamie. A member of the Board of Elders, he was also a bystander in this conversation. For whatever reason, he chose not to involve himself. If Jamie wants to make a difference in the outcome, he will have to come forward. Aware of both sides of the equation, he does not know what Pastor Ed's behavior means. He does know that the Board needs to hear Pastor Ed explain himself in a more authentic way. The words the pastor has spoken in the heat of battle have shed no light on reality as Pastor Ed sees it.

> "Hang on a moment, Noah and Pastor Ed," Jamie hesitantly began. "I'd like to take a couple of minutes and pray some about this. We're in a pretty hot argument, and generally hot arguments don't get us anywhere."

> A couple of the other elders began to nod in support as Jamie continued, "Both you, Pastor Ed, and you, Noah, have very strong feelings about this issue. It means a lot to you, Noah, that

Pastor Ed makes the calls. And as a board, we've underscored that calls are important. On the other hand, I take it that something is getting in the way of your doing what we've all agreed to do, Pastor." Both Noah and Pastor Ed nodded in agreement with this.

"Let's just ask the Holy Spirit to help us work through this," said Jamie. "And, since we know Christ is present in our midst as He has promised, we can pray for Christ to guide us as we speak. If you're willing," Jamie concluded. Everyone nodded.

With these words of invitation, Jamie took the risk of moving from someone in the role of bystander to that of an active participant. Rather than taking sides, he intervened, focusing on the process rather than the topic of the conversation. He did not ignore or deny what was actually going on. In fact, his words called attention to the intensity of the conflict, acknowledged the importance of the issue on the part of one participant (Noah), and recognized the unanswered questions on the part of the other (Pastor Ed). Noah's strategy was to create a safer space for conversation. He wanted to focus the energy of the group on solving the problem, rather than on continuing the war that someone had declared.

Further, Jamie reminded everyone that in the Body of Christ, where two or three are gathered together, there Christ is in their midst. Pointing that out was an important part of his intervention as well. Everyone in a group, especially those in Christian groups, is responsible to remind others of the presence of Christ and to pray for the blessing of the Holy Spirit.

Jamie did not press for a cheap and surface reconciliation, as if "all we really need to do is to say we are okay together." Instead, Jamie helped each participant take a step back, meditate in prayer, and center in Christ in order that deeper conversations could take place at the foot of the cross where such conversations belong. There, former combatants can more freely open up their genuine needs and concerns.

The second alternative involves either Pastor Ed or Noah. If no one else speaks up, one of these two must take the risk of venturing into unsafe territory. The self-justification must be acknowledged and stopped. One or the other leader, in humility, must confess his sins in the matter. If either Noah or Pastor Ed does that, then it may be possible for both of them to begin to listen to each other, genuinely to understand each other, to recognize that Christ has forgiven them both, and to abandon their attempts at self-justification. This is a tall order. But this is, after all, the Body of Christ.

> "Let's take a time out," suggested Noah. "I've gotten pretty worked up about this and you have too, it seems, Pastor Ed. I recognize that I'm angry with you and blaming you. We do need to get at the fact that we had an understanding about your making calls and you haven't done it. But my anger and blaming doesn't help you tell us how you see what is going on. I think you should have a place to share that, and that place is here."

> Pastor Ed quickly responded, but more quietly. "Thanks, Noah. Yes, I am pretty worked up too. I would like to have a chance to talk about the issue of my making calls. But before we do that, I'd like to apologize for my defensiveness. I was stung by what I took as criticism and tried to fight back. I was wrong, and I ask all of you to forgive me."

At this point, the group's tone and energy had completely turned around. Brothers in Christ, group members shared Christ's forgiveness with one another. Even so, they have a long way to go. Reconciliation takes a lot of work, and it most often occurs in small steps of listening and understanding over time.

> "And before we talk more about the calls," said Noah, "I'd like to suggest that we all pray together. We can take time to focus on the one who makes us a community and is present with us right now, Jesus Christ." Everyone joined hands around the table, praying in turn that Christ's presence would guide them in their discussions and decisions.

Until those involved abandon blaming one another, fractured relationships cannot be healed. To a greater or lesser extent, everyone participated in the creation of such a fracture, so everyone must participate in repairing that fracture.

How do groups prevent such fractures in the first place and heal them when they do occur? Here are some suggestions:

■ Behavioral covenants can include the processes by

which disagreements will be handled. For instance, such a covenant might say, "We agree to listen to the other person and seek to understand him/her more fully." Such an agreement makes it possible for members of the community to refer to the agreed-upon behaviors and to call attention to behaviors that lie outside the covenant.

- Then, too, a covenant can include the responses expected of the community when fractures occur. For instance, "We agree that if grievous divisions arise in which conflict has become personal, we will seek spiritual guidance and mutual forgiveness." As illustrated in the story above, this kind of agreement gives the bystanders in the group an opportunity to reference the norms that they themselves have created.

- As noted in several previous chapters, job descriptions for church workers should include expectations that are specific and behavioral. As both the worker and the relevant boards sign off on these expectations, the job description itself becomes a kind of covenant, an agreement on priorities.

- A formal evaluation process allows leaders of the community to offer feedback to the worker in a structured way.

- Congregations could undertake a study focused on healthy ways to deal with conflict in church contexts.

- Appropriate avenues for expressing grievances or concerns about the performance or attitudes of church staff need to be sanctioned and developed. Such concerns can then be addressed by the right people in healthy ways.

Most textbooks and workshops on conflict management recommend that one put aside the need to talk in order to listen to the other person. Hearing the other person out becomes more important than making one's own point. (Note: In conflicts that threaten the health or life of one or both disputants, one or both people must walk away and then find a safer time and place to talk.)

Disagreements do sometimes result in fractured relationships. More often, though, such fractures occur when disagreements are mishandled. Most people understand that others will sometimes disagree with them. But when disagreement is expressed in a deceitful, attacking, harmful, or demeaning way, then fractures are more likely to occur. Congregational leaders are responsible for managing disagreements in caring and productive ways. When fractures do occur, so must the kinds of mature, Christian behaviors that Jamie and, eventually, Noah and Pastor Ed exhibited in the story above.

The following are general tasks involved in healing fractured relationships:

- Set a tone that indicates a willingness to understand.
- Listen! Let the other person have more airtime.
- Pray freely—before, during, and after conversations.
- Pray specifically for the person with whom you are at odds.
- Own your contribution to the rift. Name it. Confess it. Ask for forgiveness.

- Remember that where two or three of Christ's followers are gathered, Christ Himself is there too.
- If things become heated, return to a posture of wanting to understand and listen to the other person.
- Take down any barriers to the Holy Spirit's work (e.g., the spirit of self-justification). Be aware of your preferred defense mechanisms and refuse to use them.
- Continue a tone that indicates you want to understand. At the same time, especially if there is a difference of opinion, be prepared to hold your ground and explore the issue fully. Healing fractured relationships does not necessarily mean compromising or abandoning your previous beliefs.
- See Christ in the other person.
- Remember that it is part of Satan's strategy to fracture relationships in the Body of Christ. Satan is the real enemy—not the other person.

SPEAKING PERSONALLY

Clearly, I can write about this a lot better than I can do it.

On my own, I lack the power to work on the healing of any fractured relationships. I, too, am often self-justifying. Like all my brothers and sisters in the faith, I throw myself on Christ, whose love and forgiveness make it possible for me to work, however feebly, toward healing.

It is Christ who continues to offer Himself to me in the Eucharist and in His Word. It is He who continues to place me in relationship with others in His Body and who strengthens me to live more peacefully within those relationships.

CHAPTER NINETEEN

WHEN PERSONALITY BECOMES THE ISSUE

"It was just a clash of personalities."

"They were just like oil and water—they never mixed."

When people talk this way, they are often talking about basic traits and characteristics. The clashes are generally more than an occasional dispute, a difference of opinion, or a dissimilar approach to problem-solving. It is "something" generic to the person that clashes with a "something else" generic to the other person.

Personality is the word we use to refer to the bundled characteristics of an individual that continue, relatively unchanged, across both time and circumstances. Each of us has a certain characteristic "way of being" that makes us who we are regardless of our immediate context. Personality is identifiable throughout our lives.

For instance, a person who is essentially neat and wants things filed away, everything in order, will likely clash with a person who is essentially scattered and tends to leave things in piles, throwing belongings around in what appears to be a disorganized fashion.

Two people who like to be in charge will likely vie for dominance when they work together on the same project. Their basic way of being is in charge, never playing second fiddle. To use another metaphor in describing this dynamic, the two will "butt heads."

Much of the time, "personality differences," especially mild ones, are accepted, understood, and even put to good use within the Body of Christ. When that happens, no significant ruptures occur. Everyone takes into account everyone else's idiosyncrasies and personal styles.

But at other times, someone's personality, his or her basic and generic "way of being," becomes problematic. When that personality is embodied in a congregational leader or in a church worker, then the whole community has a problem.

Martin Luther discusses this in his reflections on Galatians 3:

> In private persons, and even in those who hold a public office, vainglory is not as dangerous as it is in those who head the church, though in the state too, especially if vainglory befalls men in supreme command, it causes not only the disturbance and subversion of the affairs of the commonwealth but also the disturbance and change of entire kingdoms and empires, a fact to which sacred and profane histories alike testify. But when this pest slips into the church or the realm spiritual, it is impossible to tell how harmful it is; for there the contention is not about learning, intellectual endowments, beauty, riches, kingdoms, empires, etc., but either about eternal life and salvation or about eternal death and damnation.[1]

Luther's description comes quite close to what today's

psychologists might diagnose as a narcissistic personality disorder.

Personality styles lie along a continuum of harm to oneself or to others. On one end are ways of being that are helpful and useful to the community. On the other end are styles that are fracturing and destructive.

A person who tends to be more dependent and who lets others take the lead may very well be an excellent "follower" who can be counted on to meet the expectations of others. But if this person is too dependent, awaiting instructions at every turn, harm could occur when a given situation requires innovative thought. If the house is on fire, few of us wait to be told what to do by an authority. We take the initiative and move to an exit in an orderly way.

Likewise, an assertive, dominant person may take the lead. The group may count on her to be out front on every issue. But if her leadership pushes aside everyone who disagrees with her, then harm comes to both her followers and to her organization. Instead of thinking through alternatives, this leader may provoke battles over "who is in charge." This can bring harm in terms of unproductive or even wrong-headed decisions and can leave followers with wounds and scars.

Where each person in congregational leadership lies along this continuum can matter a great deal. But people do not often ask questions about it until someone's personality becomes an overt problem. At that point, it may be too late.

People knew Principal Anita was a "take charge" kind of leader. She had come to Cross of Christ's parish school with a reputation, but that was more or less what the school board wanted. They saw the former principal, Kay, as too timid and laid back. While the faculty seemed to get along with Kay pretty well, and while most members liked Kay as a person, the school had not grown. So when Kay retired, the board decided to find bolder, more assertive leadership. They wanted someone ready to take charge and move the school forward.

Principal Anita was just that kind of person. She interviewed well. She had what was seen as a winning personality; she had a history of innovating.

"Yes, she has a little 'edge' to her style," thought Naomi, the chair of the school board, "but this is just the kind of leadership that is right for us."

The entire board recommended Anita to the Voters' Assembly, and they extended a call to her as their principal.

"We did not even guess what we were getting into!" Naomi reflected to herself two years later. "We've lost two teachers—two teachers everyone else treasured! Enrollment has not grown; it's down just a little. Anita's 'edge' has caused more problems than we anticipated!"

The issues with Anita's personality had emerged within the first six months of her tenure. The board heard about emerging tensions and met with her several times, every other month at least, over the next year. Somehow, they failed to connect with her in ways that would have helped create a partnership. She seemed to take the suggestions of the board as a threat to her authority and position.

"Try as we might," Naomi mused, "We never seemed to be able to create a working partnership. Board meetings went like this:

"Member: 'We're getting some reports from parents who have tried to talk to you but felt they were simply rebuffed. They came to us, not so much complaining as wanting to heal the rift, but they feel they can't without some help.'

"Anita: 'More talking behind my back! This is a challenge to my leadership. You wanted a strong leader and you've got one. I met with the parents and told them that their ideas were wrong. That was that. You did call me to be principal. Are you going to stand with me or not?'

"Member: 'We want to stand with you, but we'd like you . . .'

"Anita: 'What is this *but* stuff?'

"Member: 'Well, there is a but. I'd like you to consider the effects of your way of interacting with parents. And we'd like to help with that.'

"Anita: 'I am who I am. If people don't like it, that's tough. And if the board doesn't like it, fire me.'

"So now," continued Naomi, thinking, "here we are at yet another school board meeting. Parents are unhappy. They have tried to work it out with Principal Anita, and she has rebuffed them. We on the board have tried to work it out with her, and have gotten nowhere. I think we may need to let her go. She is obviously not open to reflection. She's not interested in changing.

The school board is caught in a very difficult situation. Their principal's personal style and generic "way of being" is causing harm to people and to the school. If the board cannot create some kind of working alliance with Anita so she can modify her way of being principal, she will likely be released from her duties.

People in all walks of life, church workers, too, find it hard to reflect actively about their way of being. If people want to change, the task is somewhat easier. For example, a DCE struggling with depression and anxiety may want help. He can form a working alliance with congregational leaders to do that. But it is different when someone is asked to critique oneself. "Oneself" is not something a person wishes to lose. Characteristics others see as a problem cut to the core of who they are and how they behave.

Perhaps the pastor feels entitled to lord it over the congregation because of his office. Perhaps the gregarious DCE never follows through on specific tasks. Perhaps the deaconess is very inward focused and interacts with members only when she absolutely must. All these are "personality" concerns.

Cross of Christ has two alternatives: they can let the harm continue or they can dismiss Anita. Of these two alternatives, dismissal may be best. Though painful, it will protect others from harm.

A third alternative, though, would be healthier in the long run. It is the most difficult. It involves getting Anita to reflect on her way of being and to change it. But how?

First, the board needs to realize it is committing to a longer-term process. That process begins as Anita works with at least several people in the church to develop secure relationships. These people should be sanctioned for the task by those who lead or govern the church. In Principal Anita's case, for example, this could mean one or two members of the Worker Support Team, one or two members of the school board, one or two members of her faculty, and possibly other church staff.

Second, it requires a worker to commit to a self-reflective process and to ask for feedback about the impact of her behaviors and style on others. In doing so, the worker needs to risk both vulnerability and transparency. None of this is easy or painless. Some of the work may need to happen in an alternative place and space—for example, counseling, spiritual direction, or in some instances, coaching.

Many workers may resist this alternative, and understandably so. It is natural to fight when one feels embattled. This is why problems must be addressed as soon as they emerge. Conversations about the value of self-reflection are vital. Counseling or spiritual direction should be valued, sanctioned, and encouraged by the congregation or school. Cross of Christ may be willing to walk down that path with Principal Anita, but it may be too late.

After offering a fervent prayer imploring the presence of Christ in the school board meeting, Naomi began: "Principal Anita, we all know that there have been some concerns brewing of late."

Anita responded: "I've heard the concerns, and I've given them some thought."

"Let's hear your thinking about this," replied Naomi, "because we all want to find a solution to make life better for all of us. I know this has been very hard on you, Anita."

"I'm glad you recognize that," said the principal. "I know that I'm aggressive at times, and I know that I rub some people the wrong way. But I want to understand what causes me to behave in this way, and then I want to work to change it. I don't want to be a problem. I want to help people!"

"When we hired you, we thought you were right for the school. And you still bring a lot of gifts to the school," encouraged Naomi. Then she added, "Would you like a recommendation for next steps?"

"I think that's what I want," responded Anita.

"I wonder if you might consider getting some counseling. If you think of it as a consulting resource, and you want some consultation about yourself and the ways you interact with others, it might offer a great opportunity. The health insurance plan the church carries on its workers will cover most of it. There will be only a small co-pay on your part if you choose a professional in their network."

"Well," Anita said hesitantly, "I . . . okay. I'll try it."

"Great!" said Naomi. "We very much want you to do well here, and this is a great step. Thanks for your courage and openness with us."

How can congregations help their workers when personality becomes a problem? Here are a few ideas:

■ Create relationships that are as secure as possible so that transparency and vulnerability more readily become part of the relationship equation. Within relationships like that, everyone can ask for and receive feedback about the effects their personal style and behaviors have on others.

■ Utilize psychological testing to help staff and boards think together about personality style. Such instruments as the Dominance/Influence/Steadiness/Conscientiousness Profile (DISC), Myers-Briggs Trait Indicator (MBTI), and Millon Index of Personality Styles (MIPS) might be helpful. Everyone in the group should take these inventories, though, not just staff members. That way, everyone shares vulnerability.

- Intervene early. I can't say that often enough. When fissures begin to appear, address them. Do not fall prey to the temptation to dismiss them, ignore them, or placate people, while hoping things will get better. They won't.

- Remember the dominant value of helping one another in the Body of Christ. Members of the Body are in this life together. Christ Himself has brought us together. Use these truths to create momentum for growth and development.

- Remember, too, the dominant value that God's people are to be protected. If one member of the Body is consistently harming other members of the Body and is impenitent, unwilling to accept responsibility and to change, then the leadership must protect the Body as a whole. This is true even if the person causing the harm is a called worker.

SPEAKING PERSONALLY

I am annoyed with many health insurance plans when it comes to dealing with personality issues. Increasingly, such plans will pay to help treat symptoms, such as depression and anxiety, but they will often refuse to support treatment of personality disorders. Said in another way, they won't pay to help workers modify personality styles that have been proven harmful to others.

If ministry today is primarily relationship based, as I believe it is, then how I as a person affect those around me by my "way of being" becomes a very important issue. How can I learn about this without feedback? How can I learn about this without being willing to accept feedback? How can I digest and apply the feedback without having at least one other person to help me do that? Professional counselors are trained to engage clients at the deeper levels of their being.

Even if health insurance plans drop the ball on this, congregations, schools, and institutions of the church should not. Church workers need to be encouraged to grow personally; part of that growth includes growth in their own personhood.

All of us resist feedback. I would rather not look so closely at myself and the ways I affect others. I'd rather think that other people cause my problems. That means I need people around me I can trust, people who will help me and even call me to account. Congregations, schools, and other institutions of the church have a responsibility for creating an environment in which this is possible and even expected. In such a culture, everyone remains open to feedback, and that feedback is an integral part of every meeting, part of the agreed-upon covenant relationship members enjoy with one another. That way, we all learn of its value together.

CHAPTER TWENTY

ANXIETY AND DEPRESSION

Will paced back and forth in his bedroom, sweat dripping down his face. "I just can't face another person, and I just can't go to another meeting. This one coming up is just too much. The Education Committee has been on my case for months. They think I hole up in my office too much, that I should be out mixing with the youth more. They just don't understand how tough it is. They pressure me about my performance, and now they want to meet about it. I'd rather just lock the door. I feel tense all the time, and I can't sleep. Praying doesn't help. Not even Rachel knows how bad this feels."

Will continued to pace until a knock on the bedroom door broke his stride.

"What's going on?" said Rachel through the door. "You have a meeting at church. You're going to be late."

"I'm not going!" yelled Will in response.

"What?" said Rachel, as she opened the door and saw Will sitting on the bed—now in tears.

It didn't take long for Rachel to conclude Will was unable to attend the meeting. She called the church and told the committee chair, Ellen, that Will was ill.

When Ellen delivered the news to the Education Committee, the response was not good. "That does it!" said Edgar, a member of the committee. "Will is totally neglecting his responsibilities. I don't care if he is sick, he needs to be at this meeting."

"I recognize you're upset," replied Ellen, "and, frankly, I'm upset too. I was looking forward to talking with Will and trying to get to the bottom of the problem. He started out on a very positive track. I don't know what has derailed him."

"Okay," said Lilly, "we need to find a way to talk to Will and work on this together. How can we do that?"

"I think we'll need some help," suggested Ellen. "But first, how about if I arrange to talk with Will by myself as soon as he is feeling better? Perhaps with just the two of us, he'll feel less pressure. Then we can begin to think about how to proceed. I also want to consult with Jeb, the chair of the Worker Support Team. Then I think we need to involve Pastor Eli. But the first step is to find out what's going on."

While the Education Committee talked, Will sat at home with Rachel. He poured out the story of his struggles. "I'm just scared," he admitted.

"Over the past year, I've felt more and more anxious, more and more fearful before meetings. I don't want to go to work. I don't feel comfortable teaching the adult classes. It's even hard to interact with members of the Youth Group. I've tried so hard to hide it all. But I think it's finally come to a head."

Talking it through helped Will calm down. As Will calmed, so did Rachel. Still, she knew things were serious.

"Maybe now that I've talked it out, things will look better in the morning," said Will.

"I'm glad it helped to talk, Will. But we need to get some help," concluded Rachel. "Let's talk some more tomorrow."

"Sold," replied Will, "I'm too tired now."

Two things happened the next morning. Will seemed calmer as he and Rachel ate breakfast at the kitchen table. Rachel had her mind made up. "We're going to deal with this together," she informed Will. "It's been building for a long time."

"I don't want anyone to know, Rachel," said Will tentatively.

"I know it's tough, Will," Rachel continued, "but we can't do it alone. I can't do it alone."

Then the phone rang. It was Ellen. "How is Will feeling this morning?" she asked Rachel.

"Better," said Rachel, "so I'll give the phone to him."

"Hi, Ellen," began Will, "I . . . uh, I think we need to talk. There's some stuff going on that I need to share."

"Wonderful," responded Ellen. "Would it be okay if Jeb sits in too? I know he's been the point person with the Worker Support Team."

"That's good," declared Will. "I'd like Rachel to come too."

"Sure," said Ellen, "Let's set up a time for the four of us to sit down soon."

"Maybe in a week or so," suggested Will. Rachel looked at him sternly.

"Well, I take that back," said Will. "How soon can we meet?"

"I'll need to confirm this with Jeb, but let's shoot for this evening at 7:00," suggested Ellen.

"Done," agreed Will.

Will had experienced an acute anxiety attack. It apparently came as a culmination of increasing anxiety levels over the past several months. The anxiety seems to center around his responsibilities at church. What's more, his anxiety seems to be growing. That means his anxiety is becoming more and more generalized. No one has yet seen evidence that Will has tried to self-medicate with drugs or alcohol, but that is always a possibility. It is common in people who suffer from anxiety disorders.

Such disorders generally worsen over time. They do not clear up on their own. That Will has experienced more and more anxiety in the past several months indicates that the tendency will continue.

While performance issues concerned the Education Committee, Ellen sensed the need to understand more deeply. Her leadership opened up the possibility of further conversation. That conversation will likely yield better data. It will likely also create a working partnership between Will and the members of the committee. Working together, they are much more likely to find a resolution to the issues that have come up. Note that no one dismissed work performance issues. Rather, job performance became only one of a constellation of broader issues the church leaders would help Will address.

Ellen and Jeb had worked hard to build positive relationships with staff members. Happily, Will knew they had his best interests in mind. Rachel, too, would support Will and help interpret his concerns to Ellen and Jeb. Will might be tempted to keep the focus on job performance, promising to do better and agreeing to specific job-related activities. Usually, having a supportive ally present, in this case Will's wife, will help keep the focus more global and authentic.

In the end, no one backed away. Each participant, even Will, reluctant as he was, determined to address this significant problem directly and prayerfully.

Anxiety disorders are real and they are serious. Thankfully, they are also treatable. Anxiety disorders include conditions like generalized anxiety disorder, obsessive-compulsive disorder, panic disorder, agoraphobia, post-traumatic stress disorder, social anxiety disorder, and various phobias. Together, these affect over 19,000,000 people in the United States.

How can congregations help workers who develop anxiety disorders? First, leaders need to recognize the seriousness of the problem and help the worker find treatment. Here are a few other suggestions:

- It is almost impossible to overemphasize the importance of building partnerships between church leaders and staff. Had Will and Rachel not trusted Ellen and Jeb, a resolution would have come much more slowly. Meanwhile, everyone would have suffered. The strong, pre-existing relationships make it possible for everyone to work toward the same goal: better health for Will and a return to excellence in his ministry.

- Become more knowledgeable about anxiety. Resources include the Anxiety Disorders Association of America (www.adaa.org) and the American Psychological Association (www.apa.org/topics). Perhaps your church has a mental health professional who can offer resources.

- Encourage the worker to see his doctor and to make an appointment with a mental health provider. Mandate this if necessary. Generally, treatment for anxiety disorders involves counseling and perhaps medication.

- Involve the pastor. For church workers, as for all members of the Body of Christ, the spiritual dimensions of serious illness are core issues. Pastor Eli can walk through treatment with Will, using Word and Sacrament to encourage and strengthen him.

- Prepare a schedule that temporarily reduces the worker's duties. This may not apply in every case, but many workers may need it. Healing may require lessened workplace pressures for a time.

- Keep the partnership between congregation leaders, workers, and their spouses active and vibrant. This will involve ongoing, authentic conversations about the worker's progress. It will also involve holding the worker and his family up in prayer.

- Be patient. Anxiety builds up over time, and it will not resolve overnight. It can take time to find the right medication and to adjust the dosage. Since counseling should always be involved, it also will take some time to make a long-term difference. In short, there is no magic quick fix.

- Investigate the provisions for disability. If a worker's situation is so serious that it grossly interferes with his work, temporary disability may help. It will create a temporary financial safety net while the worker focuses full-time on healing. Congregations need to know the provisions and procedures of the disability insurance they provide so they can respond appropriately.

- Interpret the situation to the broader congregation,

school, or institution of the church in caring and empathic ways. Do not blame people for illness! Support them in it as Christ calls us to do.

■ Take the initiative. Anxiety disorders and other mental health problems still carry something of a stigma with many people. Shame goads many sufferers into secrecy. Often, church leaders must take an assertive posture, insisting in kind, but firm ways, that the worker get help.

Depression

Of all the mental disorders, depression is the most common. Church workers are not exempt. Like anxiety, depression is treatable, usually with a combination of counseling and medication. Since depression occurs so often in the general population, no one should find it surprising that depression is also the number one mental health issue among church workers, their spouses, and their families. The World Health Organization reports that depression affects over 121 million people worldwide. There is little doubt that depression in its various forms significantly impairs people's quality of life everywhere.

Information on depression is easily obtainable on-line from www.apa.org/topics, the National Alliance on Mental Illness (www.nami.org) or the National Institute of Mental Health (www.nimh.nih.gov).

Those suffering from depression experience low self-worth, a sense of doom, extreme fatigue, and a loss of interest in relationships and activities that once brought pleasure. Depression saps one's energy.

The Psalms describe depression in poignant terms. For example:

> Hear my prayer, O LORD;
>
> let my cry come to You!
>
> Do not hide Your face from me
>
> in the day of my distress!
>
> Incline Your ear to me;
>
> answer me speedily in the day when I call!
>
> For my days pass away like smoke,
>
> and my bones burn like a furnace.
>
> My heart is struck down like grass and has withered;
>
> I forget to eat my bread.
>
> Because of my loud groaning
>
> my bones cling to my flesh. (Psalm 102:1–5)

While some of the details differ, the ultimate effects of depression mimic anxiety in many ways. Therefore, helpful responses by congregational leaders are also similar. These include, but are not limited to, the following:

- Build a proactive partnership between congregational leaders, church workers, and their family members. Such a partnership can ease fears and open honest conversations when needs arise.

- Become more knowledgeable about depression. Mental health professionals in the congregation may offer helpful resources.

- Urge the affected worker to make an appointment for a mental health evaluation. Mandate it and accompany her to the appointment if necessary.

- Involve the pastor. Word and Sacrament ministry mean a lot to God's people during times of challenge and trouble.

- Prepare a temporary workload reduction plan for the affected worker. Depression leaves little excess energy for intense or detailed work. Investigate provisions for disability too. Depression often makes work impossible, at least in the early stages of treatment.

- Keep the partnership between church leaders and the worker active and vibrant. Communicate regularly about the worker's progress.

- Be patient. Depressive episodes do not pop up, full-blown, in a day. This illness generally develops over time. Likewise, healing takes time.

- Interpret the situation to the broader congregation, school, or organization in caring and empathic ways.

- Take the initiative. As with anxiety, depression can create feelings of shame and spur sufferers into secrecy. Often, church leaders must take an assertive posture, insisting in kind but firm ways that the worker get help.

SPEAKING PERSONALLY

Anxiety and depression are debilitating illnesses. Often, biology interacts with life events to produce these diseases. In all cases, treatment can be helpful.

Over the years, I've heard many painful stories about church members responding to a worker's anxiety or depression. I've also heard many heartwarming stories.

In general, the pain comes when congregation members treat anxiety or depression as character flaws. Workers are blamed for being lazy (in the case of depression) or not having a strong enough faith in the face of difficult circumstances (in the case of anxiety). Such blame may sound like this: "What kind of spiritual leader is he if he can't just trust God, pray, and get over it?"

The heartwarming stories, in general, grow out of empathy and understanding expressed by congregants who care about their workers and support them. Such care sounds like this: "You're not alone. This is a painful and difficult time, and I'm going to stay by your side. And so are many others in this fellowship."

Stories like these from the church workers I counsel warm my own heart and deepen my sense of the treasure God has given in the community of the faithful. Walking alongside people who suffer from anxiety and depression can be tough, but it is what God calls us to do in the Body of Christ.

CHAPTER TWENTY-ONE

ADDICTIONS

People can form addictions to many things. The most common addictions today include addictions to gambling, addictions to alcohol or drugs, addictions to pornography and sex, and addiction to the Internet and social media. Everyone, even church workers, faces the potential for addiction.

SCENE 1:

"Maybe this will be the day Lady Luck or God Almighty will look down on me with favor," thought a very anxious and worried Brenda. Brenda taught preschool at St. Matthew's Church. The preschool program offered only morning classes, so as lunch ended, Brenda walked out of the building.

"Please, God," she prayed, "make this my winning day. You've promised that whatever Your children ask in Jesus' name, You will grant. I beg You, make the slots work for me today."

Brenda had starting visiting the casino some time ago. Every so often, she would run into someone from St. Matthew's. But rarely more than once, and she could always say she was there just for an hour or so. She took special precautions to be home in time to cook dinner together with her husband, Les.

Brenda had begun with small bets, but soon discovered that making larger bets created more excitement. When the losses piled up, she bet more, trying to make up for the deficit. Les had never taken much interest in family finances; Brenda paid all the bills and managed the money. Until now, he had no idea anything was amiss.

Brenda, though, had gone from worried to desperate. "I've got to make up thousands," she thought in panic. "I'm two months behind on the mortgage and our credit card will max out in no time." She continued her prayers as she entered the casino.

"God, why don't You answer!" Brenda almost yelled as she got back into the car several hours and several major losses later. Dejected, she raced home. "Les would be really angry if he knew what was going on," she thought.

As she picked up the mail from the box, two more bills fell out. A notice from the mortgage company did too.

Not knowing what to do, Brenda went to the medicine chest and rummaged through the leftover pills. "If I took them all, then my life insurance would pay off the debts," she thought. Just then, Les came in the front door. He found

Brenda in the bathroom, the medicine chest now closed, and wondered why she looked so sad.

....

SCENE 2:

It began with a drink over lunch when the opportunity presented itself to Deaconess Stacy. It continued with a stronger drink before dinner every evening. On nights she had no meetings at King of Kings Church, Stacy poured herself several more drinks as she watched television until bedtime. When she did attend evening meetings, she always made sure to have a drink or two to unwind afterwards. Most nights, she fell into bed inebriated. But she lived alone, and no one was the wiser, or so she thought. "After all," she told herself, "St. Paul encouraged St. Timothy to take a little wine for his stomach. A little alcohol calms my soul."

"Church work can be tough," she thought to herself as she downed her third gin and tonic and poured a fourth. It was 3:00 on Saturday afternoon. She had nowhere to go, nothing to do. So why not relax?

She tried not to think about how much she drank. When she did take stock, she knew she was drinking more and more. But she always had a quick rejoinder: "I have a right to use something to settle down," she would remind herself. "Alcohol is a gift from God. The Scriptures and the Creeds both say so."

At 3:30 p.m. the phone rang. Without much thought, Stacy answered. "Deaconess Stacy, this is Lucy. My mom is in the hospital and has taken a turn for the worse. You've visited her in the assisted care center and if you can, we'd like you to come as soon as possible. She's awake and alert sometimes, but the doctors don't expect her to live more than a day or two. Could you come?"

"I'll be right there," Stacy answered, slurring her words a bit. She hung up the phone, showered, brushed her teeth, used mouthwash to remove the smell of alcohol from her breath, brushed her teeth again, drank a cup of coffee, brushed her teeth again, changed into her deaconess uniform, grabbed a couple of mints, and walked unsteadily out the door.

As she arrived at the bedside, she greeted the family members now crowded in the hospital room. She read some Scriptures, shared a few thoughts, prayed, and left.

Lucy followed the deaconess out and walked with her down the hall to the elevator. "Thanks for coming," Lucy began. "I have a question for you, though. It smells like you have been drinking. It may be none of my business, but I needed to ask." Deaconess Stacy stopped in her tracks, her eyes darting away from Lucy's gaze.

....

SCENE 3:

"I can't sleep, dear," said Pastor Jonah to his wife, Marlene.

"Anything I can do to help?" Marlene responded sleepily.

"No, I just have a lot of church issues on my mind and a bunch of things to do. I think I'll get up and do a little work. I'll be back to bed soon." He kissed Marlene, went into his home office, and flipped open his laptop.

"Too much stress, too little pleasure," thought Pastor Jonah. "And Marlene has not been feeling too well. She's never been as interested in sex as I am."

Pastor Jonah had not planned to access pornography so regularly. He had used it from time to time since high school. But only occasionally and usually with friends. It was the "guy thing" to do.

He thought getting married would curtail his use, and it did—for a while. But now, truth be told, he spent some time viewing pornography every day. And he found himself accessing materials that were more and more graphic.

He always felt guilty afterward. It was strange, at least to him. The porn compelled him beforehand, but the aftereffects felt awful. More and more, he questioned his worthiness to serve as a pastor. He hated his double life.

After a few hours, he went back to bed and fell asleep. The next morning, he grabbed his laptop and drove over to church. Docking the laptop into St. Barnabas's computer interface, he worked on Sunday's sermon. Then he left to make a few hospital and shut-in calls. As he went out the door, his secretary Becky reminded him that the computer repairperson would be in later to service everyone's equipment. Pastor Jonah didn't give it a second thought.

After three calls, he stopped for a quick, late lunch, then headed back to the office. As he walked in, he was surprised to find Peter, the head of his Board of Elders, Sam, the president of the congregation, and Becky in his office, locked in what looked like deep conversation.

"Pastor Jonah," said Sam, "we've got to talk to you about something we've found on your computer." The pastor's heart skipped a beat.

"What are you talking about?" he asked.

"You've got some very disturbing Web sites cached in your laptop's history," said Sam. "We've got to talk about this."

Something dark and destructive has these three church workers in its grasp. The force that grips them has overwhelmed both their common sense and their ethics. The causes that led to their addictions in the first place no longer matter. At this point, teacher Brenda, Deaconess Stacy, and Pastor Jonah all need help. All are engaged in a spiritual battle. All are losing.

Most congregations will find it difficult to imagine that any of their workers might be struggling with addictions this powerful. Oftentimes, church leaders react by categorizing addictions as character flaws, flaws that should lead to an automatic resignation. After all, doesn't Scripture say that spiritual leaders should be "above reproach" (1 Timothy 3:2)? Church workers who know most members will likely react this way force their addictions into ever-deeper layers of secrecy. When such addictions do finally come to light, they have grown into monsters of almost irresistible power.

Healthier congregations anticipate the struggles of all their members with sin. They know church workers share in these struggles, and they have already put a response plan in place. Healthier congregations will have:

- Set a tone of partnership and cooperation with their workers, creating a safe setting in which staff can bring concerns to the surface early.
- Put in place a Worker Support Team (WST) and established regular meetings between members of the team and the church's workers one-on-one, thus providing a specific forum for workers to share concerns.
- Offered classes on addiction led by experts in their respective fields, but also moderated by a theologically trained person, insuring that spiritual issues can surface too.

- Provided literature on addictions in the church narthex. This literature should include local resources and contact information.
- Publicized the Web sites for self-help groups and opened the church buildings for self-help group meetings: Gamblers Anonymous (www.gamblersanonymous. org), Alcoholics Anonymous (www.aa.org), Sexaholics Anonymous (www.sa.org), and Sex Addicts Anonymous (www.saa-recovery.org).

When a church worker comes forward to acknowledge an emerging or actual addiction and asks for help, congregations can:

- Establish specific accountability partnerships. Accountability to covenant agreements demands specific conversation about the addictions and the ongoing fulfillment of the agreements. Utilize specific accountability resources, such as www.xxxchurch.com for the creation of accountability concerning pornographic sites.
- Covenant with the worker to seek counseling, spiritual direction, and regular self-help group meetings. The initial counseling experience should include a professional who has specific expertise in evaluating addictions. If the health insurance the church provides for the worker does not include coverage for this, the church should find ways to help with any financial barriers to treatment.
- Covenant with married workers fully to inform the worker's spouse and to bring that person into a full

partnership so that the addiction and the resulting family fallout can be treated.

- Covenant with the worker to include regular confession and absolution as a part of the worker's spiritual direction. This confession must be specific.
- Discuss with the worker the potential need to share the struggle with judicatory officials.
- As with depression and anxiety, church leaders should research the nature of any disability coverage available to the worker. On some occasions, an addiction will have gotten such a tight hold that time away from work pressures is necessary.
- Commend the process and those involved to prayer, always remembering the goal: helping the worker.

When someone discovers a church worker's emerging or actual addiction, and that person has not voluntarily come forward, congregations need to take several steps. These apply whether or not the worker volunteers to address the problem. Some of these steps repeat the advice above, but most are additional or take on a higher level of urgency.

- Reinforce the partnership between the worker and the lay leaders of the church, particularly members of the WST. Insofar as possible, help the worker understand both intellectually and emotionally that everyone wants what is best for the worker. Even if the worker does not believe this at the time, make the WST an active and assertive player.

- Require the worker to undergo a complete psychosocial evaluation to assess the depth of the addiction and any other auxiliary concerns that support it. Then require the worker to follow the recommendations that grow out of the evaluation. These may include counseling, spiritual direction, and self-help group meetings. Use available health care insurance coverage and help with the co-pay if necessary.

- Since the worker may or may not participate willingly, make follow-through a requirement of continuing employment.

- Require that the worker's spouse be fully informed and come into partnership with the worker in battling the addiction.

- Require that confession and absolution be a regular part of the worker's spiritual direction. This confession must be specific.

- Inform regional judicatory officials of the situation and ask for their assistance. These officials may impose further requirements. Follow their lead.

- Research the nature of the worker's disability coverage. When an addiction is discovered rather than voluntarily brought forward, it is more likely that the worker will need to take some time away.

- Commend the process and those involved to prayer, remembering that the goal is to help the worker.

When an addiction has captivated a worker, leaders need to remain calm and to act in ways that reassure the rest of the church. Gathering for prayer and conversation will help, as will liberal use of the Word and Sacrament. Church members will likely see a worker who struggles with addiction in a different light. They usually expect to see their workers as more pious, as living on a higher spiritual plane than they themselves. It may even shake the faith of some to see a member of the church staff as a mere mortal, struggling with real-life issues of sin and succumbing to temptation.

Leaders need to remind one another and those who follow them that all Christians live at the foot of Christ's cross. As the old hymn puts it, each of us stands there, "just as I am, without one plea." We all share a common need for our Savior. That is only too clear! All of us are broken. And into our brokenness, Christ has come.

SPEAKING PERSONALLY

I have already mentioned growing up in an alcoholic family. Because of this, I have an insider's understanding of the many secrets addictions create. I also have an insider's understanding of the power of addictions. If left alone, the power grows until it overwhelms the addicted person and sweeps away others in their proximity.

Appeals to willpower generally accomplish nothing. They force addicts back on themselves. It doesn't help because, at that point, the power lies with the addiction, not with the person.

It's no wonder the first step in Alcoholics Anonymous is this: "We admitted we were powerless over alcohol, that our lives had become unmanageable."

The second step focuses on God, the one whom Christians know has revealed Himself in Jesus Christ. Many of the steps that follow have to do with rectifying human relationships, all the while the addict relies on the support of the AA community.

Based on all I know, I believe AA has the right process, but as a Lutheran Christian I read more specifics into that process. I know I come before God as a complete sinner. I confess my sin specifically. I receive, gladly, God's forgiveness in the person and work of Christ. He directs me to the community of the Church, to the Body of Christ, where I receive both support and accountability. Finally, He charges me as a member of that Body to help others in their struggles, not from a position of greater piety, but from a common starting point—that of our common condition as sinners.

It always moves and honors me when people ask me to help them work on the personal issues of their lives. I have come to learn how much courage it takes. I have also come to appreciate the action of the Holy Spirit in creating such courage. This is precious. I have come to be very respectful, and sometimes a bit protective, of those who do step forward to ask for help. I do not believe some authority should summarily exclude them from further ministry. Rather, in their confession, I believe we should assure them of Christ's love and forgiveness and support them as brothers and sisters in the family of God, the Body of Christ into which He has incorporated them.

Anxiety and Depression

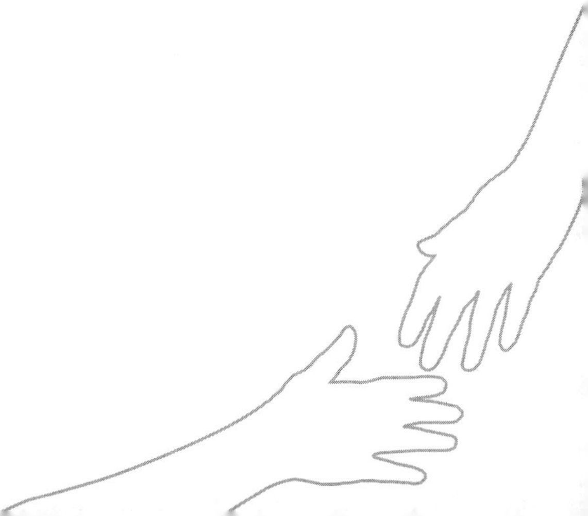

CHAPTER TWENTY-TWO

HOPES AND PRAYERS

This book has been a long time in the making. In a sense, it's been a lifetime in the making because it reflects my own personal journey in many, many ways.

I have longed to write it as I have walked through life with many church workers as their counselor or colleague. I have longed to write it as I have participated in the life of many congregations as a member or consultant. All these experiences have sensitized me to the interplay between individual workers and the institutions they have served. Again and again, I have concluded that organizations can help people stay well, and they can create toxic environments that make people sick.

My hope and prayer is that this book will contribute to the health and well-being of all who serve Christ by serving His Church. I pray that its impact goes beyond the specific suggestions I've made and that, in addition to considering these, Christian institutions look to become as healthy as they can be. From healthy organizations come healthy policies and behaviors. From healthy policies and behaviors come serious and effective supports for church staffs.

My hope and prayer is that congregations, schools, and institutions of the church will support their workers and thereby help defend them against the assaults of Satan in the following ways:

1. Churches, schools, and other Christian institutions need to recognize the vocational hazards spiritual leaders face by virtue of their calling. The more dedicated, effective, and competent a worker is, the more vulnerable that worker will be, both personally and spiritually.

■ Workers who strive to make authentic connections between the Gospel of Jesus Christ and the everyday experiences and needs of people are engaged in a spiritual battle.

■ Workers who walk closely and empathically with their people will experience the stress of their struggles, difficulties, and traumas. The more committed that walk, the more potential damage workers expose themselves to.

■ Workers who serve energetically and effectively will incur increasing life stressors.

■ Workers who bring a high level of idealism to their tasks and who want to make a difference will encounter significant temptations to disillusionment.

2. Churches, schools, and other Christian institutions need to recognize that the healthier they grow, the more support they can give to their workers. Healthy organizations understand that God has called them together to support one another. They pray and work to develop the following attitudes and build their organizational strength in the following ways:

- They grow in their identity as individuals called by God into the Body of Christ. He Himself holds them together. Individuals do not belong by accident. Christ has assembled them. They see their presence together as God's gift.
- They understand their responsibility under Christ to follow a behavioral ethic that includes truth-telling, support for one another, positive interaction, and, finally, the love first shown by Christ.
- They develop an expectation of genuine engagement and encounter. Never satisfied with outward piety, they pray and work to develop a deeper walk with one another. Real issues surface; real concerns are raised and discussed. They acknowledge and respect the skills, talents, abilities, and activities Christ has given them and others in His Body. This authenticity, love, and respect become for them a central way-of-being.
- They deliberately and strategically support the holistic experiences of their members. They avoid compartmentalizing aspects of each member's life. The organization nurtures the whole life of individual members—body, mind, and spirit.
- They create and support a Worker Support Team (WST), charging this group with the responsibility to support and advocate for church workers. The WST develops safe relationships and engages workers in significant and transparent conversations. From this context, specific strategies develop for church worker support and care.

- They initiate covenants, agreements, and promises as part of their everyday life together. They pay attention to their behaviors in light of these agreements and promises. They weave accountability into the fabric of their relationships, and give one another permission to call them to account when agreements are broken. They make liberal use of repentance, confession, and absolution.

3. Backed by good theory and research, they proactively plan strategies to support their workers' strengths and minimize their workers' vulnerabilities.

- They see the lives of their workers holistically, not compartmentalizing or expecting workers to compart-mentalize the various facets of their existence. The WST cares about and discusses all aspects of each worker's life: spiritual, emotional, vocational, social/ interpersonal, intellectual, and physical.

- They recognize the need to assess and evaluate church worker support systems. They recognize that "support" involves more than one dynamic, and they initiate systems that help workers grow professionally and emotionally. They provide interpreters to help workers better understand the culture and people to whom God has called them.

- They focus specific attention on the spiritual lives of their workers and on the spiritual armor God gives for spiritual warfare.

- They attend specifically and compassionately to matters of compensation, workload, time off, vaca-tion, Sabbath, and continuing education.

- They recognize the responsibility they carry for the health and well-being of their workers' families, and provide proactive support.
- They conduct specific conversations about concrete issues in safe settings at the foot of Christ's cross, imploring the power and blessing of the Holy Spirit.

4. When things do not go well, healthy congregations address matters directly. In doing so, they exhibit these characteristics:

- They do not ignore or deny problems and conflicts. Both are addressed specifically with the individuals involved and in a timely way.
- They provide appropriate resources workers need to address problems. Repair is the goal.
- When a problem is relational, all parties take responsibility for their part in creating and resolving it.
- When a problem is personal, the institution encourages self-awareness and openness to feedback.
- When identifiable mental health or addictive concerns surface, the institution attends to it promptly and, in Christian love, requires workers to consult skilled and competent helpers.

5. Healthy congregations always return to an understanding of who they are and whom they serve as they live out their callings in the Body of Christ, brought together and knit together by Him. They always return to an understanding of themselves, individually and collectively, as engaged in the spiritual warfare Scripture describes, embattled, but already victorious.

Realizing this, they will return again and again to the resources Christ provides: His Word, His Sacraments, and the community of the faithful that is His Body.

SPEAKING PERSONALLY

As I strive toward lifelong learning, I hope to receive feedback from my readers. You can contact me at hartungb@csl.edu. I'm especially interested in how churches, schools, individuals, and Christian institutions implement the ideas I've suggested. I very much look forward to hearing about the creative ways others in the Body of Christ have put these ideas into practice.

May this book be used well! And may church workers, their spouses, and their families, be well in Christ and in His Body.

A COVENANT OF LEADERSHIP

Our Promises to God: We promise to pray, alone and together, to thank God and to ask for God's help in our lives and in our work for our Church, and we promise to listen to God's answer to us.

Our Promises to Our Church Family: We promise to demonstrate our leadership and commitment to our Church by our example. We promise to support our Church pastors and staff so that their efforts can be most productive. We promise to try to discover what is best for our Church as a whole, not what may be best for us or for some small group in the Church.

Our Promises to Each Other: We promise to respect and care for each other. We promise to treat our time on the Board as an opportunity to make an important gift to our Church. We promise to listen with an open, non-judgmental mind to the words and ideas of others in our Church and on the Board. We promise to discuss, debate, and disagree openly in Board meetings, expressing ourselves as clearly and honestly and possible, so that we are certain that the Board understands our point of view. We promise to support the final decision of the Board, whether it reflects our view or not.

— Reprinted from *Behavioral Covenants in Congregations: A Handbook for Honoring Differences* by Gilbert R. Rendle, with permission from the Alban Institute. Copyright © 1999 by The Alban Institute, Inc. Herndon, VA. All rights reserved.

NOTES

CHAPTER 1

1. John Kleinig, "*Oratio, Meditatio, Tentatio*: What Makes a Theologian?" *Concordia Theological Quarterly* 66, no. 3 (July 2002): 265.

2. Ewald M. Plass, comp., *What Luther Says* (St. Louis: Concordia, 1959), sec. 4319.

CHAPTER 2

1. George S. Everly Jr., *A Clinical Guide to the Treatment of the Human Stress Response* (New York: Kluwer Academic, 1989), 11. Chart © George S. Everly Jr./ Kluwer Academic, adapted with permission.

2. Jonathan C. Smith, *Stress Management: A Comprehensive Handbook of Techniques and Strategies* (New York: Springer Publishing Company, Inc., 2002).

3. See Keith W. Sehnert, *Stress/Unstress: How You Can Control Stress at Home and on the Job* (Minneapolis: Augsburg, 1981).

4. Summex Health Monitor, Aggregate Report for Lutherans (2001).

5. See J. Douglas Bremmer, *Does Stress Damage the Brain?* (New York: Norton, 2002).

6. See Peter Hanson, *The Joy of Stress (Riverside, NJ: Andrews McMeel, 1987)*, 51.

CHAPTER 3

1. See Jerry Edelwich, *Burn Out: Stages of Disillusionment in the Helping Professions* (New York: Human Sciences Press, 1980), 14.

2. See John A. Sanford, *Ministry Burnout* (Ramsey, NJ: Paulist Press, 1982), 1.

CHAPTER 7

1. Thomas A. Droege, "Congregations as Communities of Health and Healing," *Interpretation* 49, no. 2 (April 1995): 117–29.

CHAPTER 8

1. Wisconsin Evangelical Lutheran Synod, *Care Committee for Called Workers* (2010), 4.

2. George Keck, *Mutual Ministry Committee* (Evangelical Lutheran Church in America, 1988), 7.

CHAPTER 9

1. For more information about a statement many churches have used successfully, see "A Covenant of Leadership" in the Appendix. I am indebted to Gilbert R. Rendle's work *Behavioral Covenants in Congregations: A Handbook for Honoring Differences* (Alban Institute, 1999). He articulates this much better than I.

2. See Association of Brethren Caregivers Staff, *The Lafiya Guide* (Elgin, IL: Association of Brethren Caregivers, 1993), 51.

3. Ewald M. Plass, comp., *What Luther Says* (St. Louis: Concordia, 1959), sec. 1160.

CHAPTER **19**

1. Ewald M. Plass, comp., *What Luther Says* (St. Louis: Concordia, 1959), sec. 3625.

ADDITIONAL RESOURCES

ADDICTIONS, ADDICTIVE BEHAVIORS

Alcoholics Anonymous, *Twelve Steps and Twelve Traditions*. New York: Alcoholics Anonymous World Services, 1981.

Carnes, Patrick, David Delmonico, and Elizabeth Griffin. *In the Shadows of the Net: Breaking Free of Compulsive Online Sexual Behavior.* Center City, MN: Hazelden, 2007.

Carnes, Patrick. *Out of the Shadows: Understanding Sexual Addiction.* Center City, MN: Hazelden, 2001.

Gamblers Anonymous. www.gamblersanonymous.org.

Sex Addicts Anonymous. www.saa-recovery.org.

Sexaholics Anonymous. www.sa.org.

BURNOUT, STRESS, TRAUMA

Abramson, Alexis. *The Caregiver's Survival Handbook: How to Care for Your Aging Parents without Losing Yourself.* New York: Berkley Publishing, 2004.

Aronson, Elliot, and Ayala Pines. *Burnout: from Tedium to Personal Growth.* New York: Free Press, 1981.

———. *Career Burnout: Causes and Cures.* New York: Free Press, 1988.

Baab, Lynne M. *Beating Burnout in Congregations.* Bethesda: Alban Institute, 2003.

Cherniss, Cary. *Beyond Burnout: Helping Teachers, Nurses, Therapists, and Lawyers Recover From Stress and Disillusionment.* New York: Routledge, 1995.

Figley, Charles R., ed. *Treating Compassion Fatigue.* New York:

Brunner-Routledge, 2002.

Grady, Denise. "Sudden Stress Breaks Hearts, a Report Says." *New York Times* (February 10, 2005): Health Section.

Herman, Judith L. *Trauma and Recovery: The Aftermath of Violence from Domestic Abuse to Political Terror.* New York: Basic Books, 1997.

Horowitz, Mardi J. *Stress Response Syndromes.* Northvale, NJ: Jason Aronson Inc., 1986.

Kahn, Ada P. *Stress A–Z: A Sourcebook for Facing Everyday Challenges.* New York: Checkmark Books, 2000.

Klarreich, Samuel H. *Work without Stress: A Practical Guide to Emotional and Physical Well-being on the Job.* New York: Brunner/Mazel Publishers, 1990.

Lovallo, William R. *Stress and Health: Biological and Psychological Interactions.* Thousand Oaks, CA: SAGE Publications, 2005.

McEwen, Bruce. *The End of Stress As We Know It.* Washington DC: Joseph Henry Press, 2002.

McVicker, Barbara, and Darby McVicker Puglielli. *Stuck in the Middle: Shared Stories and Tips for Caregiving Your Elderly Parents.* Bloomington, IN: Author House, 2008.

Nelson, Debra, James Quick, and Jonathan Quick. *Stress and Challenge at the Top: The Paradox of the Successful Executive.* New York: John Wiley and Sons, 1990.

Rediger, G. Lloyd. *Coping With Clergy Burnout.* Valley Forge: Judson Press, 1982.

Roskies, Ethel. *Stress Management for the Healthy Type A: Theory and Practice.* New York: Guilford Press, 1987.

Rothschild, Babette. *Help for the Helper: The Psychophysiology of Compassion Fatigue and Vicarious Trauma.* New York: W.W. Norton and Company, 2006.

Smith, Jonathan C. *Stress Management A Comprehensive Handbook of Techniques and Strategies.* New York: Springer Publishing, 2002.

Stamm, B. Hudnall, ed. *Secondary Traumatic Stress: Self-Care*

Issues for Clinicians, Researchers, and Educators. Baltimore: Sidran Press, 1999.

Van der Kolk, Bessel A., Alexander McFarlane, and Lars Weisaeth, eds. *Traumatic Stress: The Effects of Overwhelming Experience on Mind, Body, and Society.* New York: Guilford Press, 2007.

Zal, H. Michael. *The Sandwich Generation: Caught between Growing Children and Aging Parents.* New York: Perseus Publishing, 1992.

CHURCH WORKER HEALTH AND SELF-CARE

Eppley, Harold, and Rochelle Melander. *The Spiritual Leader's Guide to Self-Care.* Bethesda, MD: Alban Institute, 2002.

Gills, James P. *Temple Maintenance: Excellence with Love.* Tarpon Springs, FL: St. Luke's Cataract and Intraocular Lens Institute, 1989.

Halaas, Gwen W. *The Right Road: Life Choices for Clergy.* Minneapolis: Fortress Press, 2004.

Oswald, Roy M. *Clergy Self-Care: Finding A Balance for Effective Ministry.* Washington DC: Alban Institute, 1991.

Rediger, G. Lloyd G. *Fit to Be a Pastor: A Call to Physical, Mental, and Spiritual Fitness.* Louisville, KY: Westminster John Knox Press, 2000.

Richardson, Ronald W. *Becoming a Healthier Pastor: Family Systems Theory and the Pastor's Own Family.* Minneapolis: Fortress Press, 2005.

Tuggle, Melvin. *It is Well with My Soul: Churches and Institutions Collaborating for Public Health.* Washington DC: American Public Health Association, 2000.

Wheat Ridge Ministries, *Health Ministry Self-Study for Congregations,* http://www2.wheatridge.org/resources/slfstudy.shtml.

CHURCH WORKER STRUGGLES

Bowers, Margaretta K. *Conflicts of the Clergy: A Psychodynamic Study with Case Histories.* New York: Thomas Nelson & Sons, 1964.

Coate, Mary Anne. *Clergy Stress: The Hidden Conflicts in Ministry.* London: SPCK, 1989.

Edmondson, Robert, and Gary McIntosh. *It Only Hurts on Monday: Why Pastors Quit and What You Can Do about It.* Carol Stream, IL: ChurchSmart Resources, 1998.

Gaddy, C. Welton. *A Soul under Siege: Surviving Clergy Depression.* Louisville, KY: Westminster John Knox Press, 1991.

Gram, Harold, and James Gram. *The Devil Never Walks Alone.* Coral Springs, FL: Llumina Press, 2005.

Klaas, Alan, and Cheryl Klaas. *Quiet Conversations: Concrete Help for Weary Ministry Leaders.* Kansas City, MO: Mission Growth Publications, 2000.

Lehr, Fred. *Clergy Burnout: Recovering from the 70-Hour Work Week and Other Self-Defeating Practices.* Minneapolis: Fortress Press, 2006.

Rassieur, Charles L. *Stress Management for Ministers: Practical Help for Clergy Who Deny Themselves the Care They Give to Others.* Philadelphia: Westminster Press, 1982.

Rogers, Tom. *Life in the Fishbowl: Building Up Church Workers.* St. Louis: Concordia, 1996.

Sloat, Donald. *Growing Up Holy and Wholly: Understanding and Hope for Adult Children of Evangelicals.* Brentwood, TN: Wolgemuth & Hyatt Publishers, 1990.

CHURCH WORKER SUPPORT

Bullock, A. Richard, and Richard J. Bruesehoff. *Clergy Renewal: The Alban Guide to Sabbatical Planning.* Bethesda, MD: Alban Institute, 2000.

Division of News and Information, LCMS Communications. Pressure Points. *Reporter.* The Lutheran Church—Missouri Synod, 1991–2011.

Duey, William J. "Church Worker Growth and Support, Commission on Ministerial Growth and Support." *Reporter,* August 2004.

Galloway, John Jr. *Ministry Loves Company: A Survival Guide for Pastors.* Louisville, KY: Westminster John Knox Press, 2003.

Gottman, John M. *The Relationship Cure: A Five-Step Guide to Strengthening Your Marriage, Family, and Friendships.* New York: Three Rivers Press, 2001.

Kuntz, Arnold. *Keeping the Servant Spark: Encouragement for Christian Caregivers.* St. Louis: Concordia, 1992.

Miller, Susan. *After the Boxes Are Unpacked: Moving On After Moving In.* Colorado Springs: Focus on the Family, 1995.

Moon, Gary W., and David G. Benner, eds. *Spiritual Direction and the Care of Souls: A Guide to Christian Approaches and Practices.* Downers Grove, IL: InterVarsity Press, 2004.

Nichols, Michael P. *The Lost Art of Listening: How Learning to Listen Can Improve Relationships.* New York: The Guilford Press, 2009.

Nuechterlein, Anne Marie. *Improving Your Multiple Staff Ministry: How to Work Together More Effectively.* Eugene, OR: Wipf and Stock Publishers, 2000.

Purushotham, Gwendolynn. *Watching over One Another in Love: A Wesleyan Model for Ministry Assessment.* Nashville: General Board of Higher Education and Ministry the United Methodist Church, 2007.

Reber, Robert, and D. Bruce Roberts. *A Lifelong Call to Learn: Continuing Education for Religious Leaders.* Herndon, VA: Alban Institute, 2010.

Wisconsin Evangelical Lutheran Synod, Care Committee for Called Workers. Wisconsin Evangelical Lutheran Synod, 2010.

Wuellner, Flora S. *Feed My Shepherds: Spiritual Healing and Renewal for Those in Christian Leadership.* Nashville: Upper Room Books, 1998.

CONGREGATIONAL LIFE
AND ORGANIZATIONAL DYNAMICS

Bonhoeffer, Dietrich. *Life Together.* New York: HarperOne, 1954.

Bullard, George W. Jr. *Every Congregation Needs a Little Conflict.* St. Louis: Chalice Press, 2008.

Comella, Patricia, et al, eds. *The Emotional Side of Organizations: Applications of Bowen Theory.* Washington DC: The Georgetown Family Center, 1995.

Fassel, Diane, and Anne Schaef. *The Addictive Organization.* San Francisco: Harper and Row, 1988.

Friedman, Edwin. *Generation to Generation: Family Process in Church and Synagogue.* New York: Guilford Press, 1985.

Hale, W. Daniel, and Harold Koenig. *Healing Bodies and Souls: A Practical Guide for Congregations.* Minneapolis: Fortress Press, 2003.

Hanson, Laurie, and Ivy Palmer eds. *Pastor and People: Making Mutual Ministry Work.* Minneapolis: Augsburg Fortress, 2003.

Miller, Herb. *Church Personality Matters: How to Build Positive Patterns.* St. Louis: Chalice Press, 1999.

Olsen, Charles M. *The Wisdom of the Seasons: How the Church Year Helps Us Understand Our Congregational Stories.* Herndon, VA: Alban Institute, 2009.

Rediger, G. Lloyd. *Clergy Killers: Guidance for Pastors and Congregations under Attack.* Louisville, KY: Westminster J. Knox Press, 1997.

———. *The Toxic Congregation: How to Heal the Soul of Your Church.* Nashville: Abingdon Press, 2007.

Rendle, Gilbert R. *Behavioral Covenants in Congregations: A*

Handbook for Honoring Differences. Bethesda, MD: Alban Institute Publication, 1999.

Richardson, Ronald W. *Creating a Healthier Church: Family Systems Theory, Leadership, and Congregational Life.* Minneapolis: Fortress Press, 1996.

Vaill, Peter B. *Learning as a Way of Being: Strategies for Survival in a World of Permanent White Water.* San Francisco: Jossey-Bass Inc., 1996.

LEADERSHIP

Berry, Erwin. *The Alban Personnel Handbook for Congregations.* Bethesda, MD: Alban Institute Publication, 1999.

Blanchard, Kenneth H. *The One Minute Manager.* New York: Berkley Books, 1983.

Carroll, Jackson W. *God's Potters: Pastoral Leadership and the Shaping of Congregations.* Grand Rapids: Eerdmans, 2006.

Friedman, Edwin, E. W. Beal, et al. *A Failure of Nerve: Leadership in the Age of the Quick Fix.* New York: Seabury Books, 2007.

Friedman, Edwin. *Friedman's Fables.* New York, Guilford Press, 1990.

Lencioni, Patrick. *The Five Dysfunctions of a Team: A Leadership Fable.* San Francisco, Jossey-Bass, 2002.

———. *Silos, Politics and Turf Wars: A Leadership Fable about Destroying the Barriers that Turn Colleagues into Competitors.* San Francisco, Jossey-Bass, 2006.

Marcuson, Margaret J. *Leaders Who Last: Sustaining Yourself and Your Ministry.* New York: Seabury Books, 2009.

McIntosh, Gary. and Samuel Rima. *Overcoming the Dark Side of Leadership.* Grand Rapids: Baker Books, 1997.

NEUROSCIENCE

Berns, Gregory. *Iconoclast: a Neuroscientist Reveals How to Think*

Differently. Boston: Harvard Business School Press, 2008.

Cozolino, Louis J. *The Neuroscience of Human Relationships: Attachment and the Developing Social Brain.* New York: Norton Press, 2006.

Goddard, Sally. *A Teacher's Window into the Child's Mind: A Non-Invasive Approach to Solving Learning and Behavior Problems.* Eugene, OR: Fern Ridge Press, 1996.

Hannaford, Carla. *The Dominance Factor: How Knowing Your Dominant Eye, Ear, Brain, Hand & Foot Can Improve Your Learning.* Arlington, VA: Great Ocean Publishers, 1997.

Larsen, Stephen. *The Healing Power of Neurofeedback.* Rochester, VT: Healing Arts Press, 2006.

MacLean, Paul. *A Triune Concept of the Brain and Behavior.* Toronto and Buffalo: University of Toronto Press, 1973.

Minton, Kekuni, Pat Ogden, and Clare Pain. *Trauma and the Body: A Sensorimotor Approach to Psychotherapy.* New York: W.W. Norton and Company, 2006.

Siegel, Daniel J. *The Developing Mind: Toward a Neurobiology of Interpersonal Experience.* New York: The Guilford Press, 1999.

———. *The Mindful Brain.* New York: Norton Press, 2007.

PROFESSIONAL ASSOCIATIONS AND SUPPORT ORGANIZATIONS

American Association of Pastoral Counselors, www.aapc.org.

American Psychological Association, www.apa.org.

Anxiety Disorders Association of America, www.adaa.org.

Christianity Today International, www.christianitytoday.com; see also leadershipjournal.net.

Doxology: The Lutheran Center for Spiritual Care and Counsel.,http://www.doxology.us.

Grace Place: Lutheran Wellness Ministries, http://graceplaceretreats.org.

Healthy Congregations, www.healthycongregations.com.
Lombard Mennonite Peace Center, www.lmpeacecenter.org.
National Alliance on Mental Illness, www.nami.org.
National Institute of Mental Health, www.nimh.nih.gov.
Peacemaker Ministries, www.peacemaker.net.
Stephen Ministries, www.stephenministries.org.
Wellness Council of America, www.welcoa.org.
Wellspring, www.wellspring.net.
Wheat Ridge Ministries, www.wheatridge.org.
Whole Person Associates, www.wholeperson.com.

Psychological and Leadership Skills Testing

Alban Institute. Building Up Congregations & Their Leaders, www.alban.org.

Baab, Lynne M. *Personality Type in Congregations: How to Work with Others More Effectively*. Bethesda, MD: Alban Institute, 1998.

BridgeBuilders International. Leadership Network, www.bridge-builders.org.

Dominance/Influence/Steadiness/Conscientiousness Profile, www.discprofile.com.

Myers-Briggs Trait Indicator (MBTI), www.myersbriggs.org.

Spiritual Warfare

Cooper, Terry, and Cindy Epperson. *Evil: Satan, Sin and Psychology*. New York: Paulist Press, 2008.

Farley, Edward. *Good and Evil: Interpreting a Human Condition*. Minneapolis: Fortress Press, 1990.

Jacobs, Alan. *Original Sin: A Cultural History*. New York: HarperOne, 2008.

Wiley, Tatha. *Original Sin: Origins, Developments, Contemporary*

Meaning. New York: Paulist Press, 2002.

THEOLOGICAL AND BIBLICAL RESOURCES

Kleinig, John. "*Oratio, Meditatio, Tentatio*: What Makes a Theologian?" *Concordia Theological Quarterly* 66, no. 3 (July 2002).

Ludwig, Garth. *Order Restored: A Biblical Interpretation of Health, Medicine, and Healing.* St. Louis: Concordia Academic Press, 1999.

Luther, Martin. *Luther's Small Catechism with Explanation.* St. Louis: Concordia, 1986, 1991.

———. *What Luther Says.* Compiled by Ewald M. Plass. St. Louis: Concordia, 2006.

Nygren, Anders. *Commentary on Romans.* Philadelphia: Muhlenberg Press, 1949.

Scharlemann, Martin. *Healing and Redemption.* St. Louis: Concordia, 1965.